Patrick J Flatley

Ireland And the Land League

Patrick J Flatley

Ireland And the Land League

ISBN/EAN: 9783744724128

Printed in Europe, USA, Canada, Australia, Japan

Cover: Foto ©ninafisch / pixelio.de

More available books at **www.hansebooks.com**

IRELAND AND THE LAND LEAGUE.

KEY

TO

THE IRISH QUESTION.

By P. J. FLATLEY, Esq.

WITH AN INTRODUCTION

BY

Hon. WENDELL PHILLIPS.

BOSTON:
PUBLISHED BY D. O'LOUGHLIN & CO.,
No. 630 Washington Street.
1881.

INTRODUCTION.

The Irish question is daily attracting more and more notice. It is, indeed, the pivot on which, just now, English politics turn. Meanwhile, it is a question in regard to which very few men have accurate information; and the sources from which this is obtained are widely scattered, and not easily reached.

The discussions, in journals and speeches, necessitate a constant reference to trustworthy sources, and are often comparatively worthless from the lack of exact and accurate statements and statistics. The reader needs also to know something of the legislation, which, during the last century, has resulted in the present condition of the oppressed peasantry. Tables of statistics, respecting crime, population, wealth, rents, division of land, education, etc., etc., are absolutely necessary, if one would correctly estimate the causes that have been at work, the evils which have resulted, and the value of the different measures and methods of relief proposed. Extracts from the speeches of the leaders in the Land League movement, giving trustworthy information of what they wish done, and how they intend to get it done, are the only fair basis on which to discuss and criticise their acts and words.

Any Manual containing such items of information must be of great value to the fair-minded journalist who takes part in this discussion; to the speaker who wishes to have at hand the authority for his statements and the basis of his arguments; and to the general inquirer who seeks to study this question dispassionately and thoroughly.

The author of the following pages has sought to meet this want, and to supply, from the most trustworthy sources, precisely that kind of information to which we have alluded. He offers these pages to the friends of the cause as ammunition for their use in this agitation; and to the critics and enemies of the movement, as a challenge and test-measure by which to judge of the objections they so groundlessly urge and blindly insist upon.

Mr. Flatley has aimed to make the work accurate and trustworthy, and to give as complete information as possible, so as to enable the reader to become master of the question.

The sun of Ireland was never so near its

noon. The success of the present agitation has been wonderful. It is rare proof of the ability of Parnell and his helpers that, with such slight means, they have been able to accomplish so much. He has watched his opportunity and seized with masterly ability every possible chance of arresting public attention and compelling the government to listen to his claim. And never before has there been so much progress made in twenty months.

Four years ago you could hardly keep a quorum in the House of Commons if the Irish question was in debate; the press ignored it, and readers were generally weary of listening to Ireland's claims. But within two years, without using any means which are not strictly parliamentary, keeping within the limits of legal and honorable agitation, Parnell has filled all the leading journals, here and in Europe, with articles on the Irish question; he has loaded down the Reviews and Magazines with discussions and controversies touching Ireland; Parliament has become only an Irish debating society; the civilized world pauses to gaze on the struggle going on in Great Britain between a landed aristocracy threatened with ruin and the masses rising to claim that they be lifted to the level of the nineteenth century, where France, Belgium, Germany, and Russia stand; and when an emperor is assassinated men's minds turn instantly to ask, What effect will it have on the Irish question?

One remarkable feature of the present agitation, distinguishing it from all previous ones, is that all classes, all sects, and every district in the Island are united in this effort to throw off the cruel yoke. Protestant stands side by side with Catholic; Celt rallies to the side of Saxon, northern Scottish and western pure Irish blood, all put willing and hearty hands to this plough in the glad hope that it will tear out every root of bitterness, and leave Ireland contented, prosperous, and united.

It seems now only necessary that Ireland's friends here should be united, and success must be ours. These moral movements do not seemingly accomplish quickly as much as the sword appears to do. But half of what the sword gains is lost when the fury of the contest abates and society cools down to its usual mood. On the other hand, all that peaceful agitation puts into the statute book remains forever — a step once gained is gained forever.

If the friends of Ireland will stand resolutely shoulder to shoulder, and let no dissensions creep in to weaken their ranks, I look for a practical settlement of this question within a very few years, and confidently expect to see so much wrung from Parliament as to secure the surrender of all the rest of our claim, whenever the next movement takes place along our lines.

The events of the day, the civilization of the age, all tending to weaken the crippling land system which still lingers in Great Britain; the convulsions in all the European states, their foundations honeycombed by discontent; the wealth, and moral and political influence of the Irish race in this country,—all these elements used with consummate skill and the utmost fidelity by leaders who have the ear of the world,—these are guarantees of victory if we will be only active, united, and true.

WENDELL PHILLIPS.

IRELAND AND THE LAND LEAGUE.

The object of this volume is to quarry, if not polish, one stone for the temple of Irish liberty. And this it proposes to do by giving a *résumé* of the necessity, inception, and prospects of the Irish National Land League. Many are ignorant of the reasons for the faith that is in us, know not what manner of men we land-leaguers are, feel uncertain of the necessity of the movement; and it is to clear away all misapprehension on these and kindred subjects that this publication seeks the light. To perform this work we must, in part, reproduce the past, photograph, as best we can, the present, and throw, so far as we may, some seer-like views on the future. To comprehensively perform this is not, in the nature of things, possible within the time and limits at our disposal; but we shall not set down aught in malice, and for every statement made needing proof, there shall be abundant evidence furnished in the appendix attached.

To a traveller from the United States visiting Europe, the first land that gladdens his view emerging from the bosom of the waters, with sea-gulls hovering over its cliffs, and the white waves caressing its beach, is that island of marvellous verdure — Ireland. We may not linger on the fanciful derivations of its name; yet it is, like most other names, one of much significance. Ireland is divided by St. George's Channel, forty-seven miles in breadth, from England. It has a superficial area of thirty-two thousand five hundred miles; that is, over twenty millions of acres of land, nearly three millions of which are unimprovable. It is divided into four provinces — Ulster, to the north, containing nine counties; Munster, to the south, containing six counties; Leinster, to the east, containing twelve counties; and Connaught, to the west, containing five counties. The population is about five millions and a half, five-sixths being farmers and laborers, with their wives and families, engaged in the cultivation of the soil; so that agriculture is the only substantial industry of the country.

To understand intelligently the present great problem that presses for solution, we should know something of early Irish institutions. From a far-past age the Irish had a system of jurisprudence, and it was customary to hold triennial assemblies of the people. Six years after their conversion to Christianity, and at one of those assemblies held at Tara, a commission was appointed to revise the laws. This commission consisted of three Kings, three Bishops, and three Brehons or Judges; and they submitted a report in 341, three years after their appointment. This report or digest was titled "Senchus Mor," and was formally ratified and adopted as the supreme law of the land, and continued respected and recognized throughout the country (with the exception of that part called the "Pale") until the beginning of the seventeenth century. Sir Henry Sumner Maine, in his "Early History of Institutions," writes: "It is true, as I said before, even of the BREHON law, that it does not wholly disappoint the patriotic expectations entertained of it. When they are disencumbered of archaic phrase and form, there are some things remarkably modern in it. I quite agree with one of the editors, that in the ancient Irish law of civil wrong there is a singularly close approach to modern doctrines on the subject of contributory negligence; and I have found it possible to extract from the quaint texts of the Book of Aicill some extremely sensible rulings on the difficult subject of the measure of damages, for which it would be vain to study the writings of Lord Coke, though these last are relatively of much later date. But the Brehon law pays heavily for this apparent anticipation of the modern legal spirit. It must be confessed that most of it has a strong air of fancifulness and unreality."

Despite this charge of fancifulness, which is partially true, the "Senchus Mor" is a wonderful compilation of principles and rules applicable to all kinds of property, and setting forth the various forms of pleading. With regard to the land, it was held in the name of the chief for the benefit of the tribe, the right of alienation rested with the tribe, and no free member could be ousted from occupancy. Slavery existed in Ireland at that time; but the humane temper of the people is seen by the provisions made for the well-being of the slave. The chief's honor would be tarnished by injuring the slave, as much as if he did injury to his son or to his wife. Emancipation was not infrequent, and then the slave became a base-tenant, under obligation to pay rent in kind. In case of charging an excessive rent the chief was liable to a fine. Land acquired by purchase might be sold without requiring outside ratification, and ownership of property for a fixed period of time conferred a certain degree of nobility. It was provided too that "every one is ruler of his own land, whether it be small or whether it be large." This evidently refers to the free tenants. Under this system the Irish people, rich in flocks and herds — for there was little or no money in circulation — had lived and flourished from a time anterior to the foundation of Rome; when, as with the rapidity of a prairie fire, the country was invaded by Henry the Second and his myrmidons. Without any plea of right, or any pretence of justice, he parcelled out the whole island among ten of his doughty followers; they in turn were to subdivide it. To inquire into the causes of their coming has no interest for us other than to know that they had a hunger for possession of the land. Henry claimed to be " Lord Paramount " of Ireland, and no other title was assumed by his successors until, in 1542, Henry the Eighth was declared to be king by a fawning Parliament, convened for that purpose.

Meanwhile, what had been accomplished for the assimilation of both races during the four centuries? Save intermarriages between the Norman chiefs and daughters of Irish chieftains, practically nothing. A small strip called the " Pale," consisting of Dublin, Louth, Kildare, Waterford and some walled cities was held by the English: there English law was enforced. Outside that limit the Brehon law, Irish customs and usages were in full force. Repeatedly had some of the Irish asked for the benefit of the

English law, and as often was it refused save to those "of the Five Bloods." If an Irishman peaceably seeking his home after a day's labor in the fields was assailed and shot by an Englishman, when the case came for trial within the "Pale" the simple defence that the man slain was a "mere Irishman" was sufficient to acquit the prisoner. This naturally provoked reprisals. Outside the "Pale" in such a case an eric or fine would be imposed, the amount determined by the social standing of the victim, for capital punishment was almost unknown in the Brehon code.

The Irish were a very musical people. Giraldus Cambrensis, who visited Ireland during the time of Henry the Second, says that in music this people surpassed all the nations of Europe. Nearly two hundred years after the invasion, the statute of Kilkenny, enacted in 1367, enumerates six different classes of minstrels, made it penal to entertain them, and forbade them to enter the "Pale" under pain of imprisonment. Those who know how the ministry of music refines the manners and elevates the thought, can form their own conclusions as to the æsthetic character of both peoples. Were they to remain two, or would Henry the Eighth, who had a little experience in weddings, have them both united and married to the soil? He could not play such a *rôle*. Conscience forbade his recognition as spiritual king, and so no banns could be published just yet. His son was too much of a weakling to accomplish anything. Elizabeth wielded the hammer of Thor in crushing the Irish. She sent her sternest generals there: the greater the ruin the greater her glee. Some of her best officers never saw her again. —— She was titled the " Virgin Queen." But no laughing grace, no swan-like pose, no soul-speaking face, no witching loveliness can be seen in her inflated majesty. We may visit another member of the family, yonder, in Fotheringay, and there see these and a hundred other charms in full blossom. But Elizabeth is angered at the contrast, no less than at the stubborn " Irishrie," who have sent back the favorite Essex with withered laurels from the " Pass of Plumes." She will sign the death-warrant of her kinswoman, Mary Queen of Scots, and would fain do the same for gallant Red Hugh, and the majestic O'Neil, who, like a whirlwind, sweep over the English hosts at Beal a-na-buie. And now she raves, nay, swears, unroyal, unwomanly though it be. The flower of her troops is in Ireland; the Spanish fleet in the offing; its admiral not wisely selected for the work to be done. The Irish are beaten in the fight, and on their retreat pass over the grounds of the Earl of Desmond, 573,000 acres, confiscated some sixteen years before. It is now, under her royal proclamation, occupied by "undertakers," "none of the native Irish to be admitted." Among the beneficiaries is Sir Walter Raleigh, who received forty-two thousand acres, and another of no less fame, the author of the "Faerie Queen," who received three thousand acres, with the castle of Kilcolman, on the banks of the Mulla. Edmund Spenser reserved the charities of his nature for the home circle, and creatures of imagination, else his castle would not be given to the flames, his son burned to death, and he himself forced to fly to London with some cantos of his masterpiece as his only property. Before this terrible devastation in Munster, Shan Burke's country was visited, and Ulick Burke's country, both in Connaught, visited in like manner by Sir Richard Bingham — "The Devil's reaping-hook." "He consumed with fire and sword, sparing neither old nor young." O'Neil, pursued like a stag by the hounds, was at length brought to bay. Honorable terms of capitulation were given him, and the articles had scarce been signed when the news came that Elizabeth had breathed her last.

Then new hope sprang up in the hearts of the Irish people. The memory of the mother, it was thought, would move the son to grant large concessions to the Irish. These hopes were doomed to disappointment. The same bitterness of feeling anent the politico-religious fight was kept alive, and in a few years a trumped-up charge of conspiracy was made against O'Neil and his brother chieftains. A letter had been found, implicating them, it was alleged, in some disloyal practices. He had been trained and educated in England, and felt they were weaving a web to ensnare the valiant remnant of a once chivalrous army. With soldier steadiness the resolution was taken, and they sailed from a land that contains no prouder monument of martial glory than the record they left behind. On the continent they were received with almost royal honors, and ever sighed to come back again and cross blades with the enemy. This they expected to carry out with foreign aid; but such aid, though a good crutch, is seldom a good leg to stand on. Moreover, the Continent trembled with the rumblings of conflict from anear. The Thirty Years' War threw its shadow before, and nations friendly to Ireland whet their weapons for defence or aggression. So it was that the aid relied on never came. Weary waiting for the day of freedom for their country, the sacred exiles found everlasting deliverance for their own souls. The manner of the death of one only was melancholy in the extreme; that of O'Sullivan Beare, boldest lion of them all, laid low by the dagger of an English assassin in the streets of Madrid.

By the departure of the chiefs the plans of King James for a "plantation" were successful. Not, however, under the Brehon code, for according to this members of the clan could not, by attainder of their chiefs, lose their property in the soil; so the clansmen felt wroth and angry, and the old law of their forefathers, revised nearly twelve hundred years before, was now abolished forever. James felt it incumbent on him to write to his royal brothers in Europe, a statement, dated Nov. 15, 1607, in justification of the steps he had taken; but what importance they attached to it may be estimated by the fact that they treated their distinguished Irish guests with still greater kindness and consideration. That the letter implicating them in the conspiracy was a mere decoy is proved by papers of Lord Bacon, suggesting the best method of "plantation," and bearing date long before the flight of the earls. The national spirit, even at this dark moment, was not wholly extinguished. A diversion was made by Sir Cahir O'Doherty, prince of Irishowen. He seized the town of Derry, carried on a guerilla warfare for some months, and fell fighting at the head of his troops. The movement then collapsed. James confiscated six counties, containing two millions of acres, and, determined to exclude the original owners, he invited his English and Scotch subjects to take possession of Tyrone, Derry, Donegal, Armagh, Fermanagh, and Cavan. A committee appointed to investigate the nature of the soil, reported: "The country is well watered, generally by an abundance of springs, brooks, and rivers; and plenty of fuel, either by means of wood, or where that is wanting, of good and wholesome turf. It yieldeth store of all necessaries for man's sustenance, in such measures as may not only maintain itself, but also furnish the city of London yearly with manifold provisions, especially for their fleets, namely, with beef, pork, fish, rye, bere, peas and beans, which will, also, in some years, help the dearth of the city and country about, and the store-houses appointed for the relief of the poor. As it is fit for all sorts of husbandry, so for breeding of mares and increase of cattle it doth excel, whence may be expected butter, cheese, hides, and tallow. . . . English sheep will breed abundantly in Ireland, the sea-coast and the nature of the soil being very wholesome for them. . . . It affordeth fells of all sorts in great quantity: red deer, foxes, sheep, lambs, rabbits, martens, squirrels, etc. . . . Hemp and flax do more naturally grow there than elsewhere. . . . The country is very plentiful for honey and wax."

It would be a bootless task to go over the work of the commission appointed by the king, for their report was a foregone conclusion: it was simply to give a colorable title of right to his Majesty's legalized robbery.

The "undertakers," principally Scotch, became owners of the soil for little more than a nominal consideration. The conditions attached to the conveyance were that castles and bawns should be built, and all measures taken to render them more secure; chiefly that themselves, their heirs or assigns, should not alien or demise their portions, or any part thereof, to the "meer Irish." The English devil-fish threw its tentacles over the richest and most fertile part of Ulster; the evicted owners might take to the bog or the mountain. Their leaders can aid them no more, nor hear the voice of their mourning. But in each mountain fastness they nurse an angry spirit of revenge, and ill brook the sight of the stranger lording it in the homes of their fathers. Their great chieftain, third of the military captains of the age in the opinion of the king of France, is called a "Traitor" by the English.

> "How many a spirit born to bless,
>   Did fall beneath that with'ring name,
> Whom but a day's, an hour's success,
>   Had wafted to eternal fame."

Yes; but one day's success against Carew, at that supreme crisis, and thy name, Hugh O'Neil, would have floated down the centuries a talisman of power for every downtrodden people. For thy countrymen at home and abroad it has still the force of a spell, to —— But, no matter, it shall be graven on their memories forever.

Meantime, Charles the First succeeds to

the throne, and seeks to replenish his exchequer by confiscations in Ireland. The English Parliament refuse to make the required appropriations; and, straitened for funds, Charles promises to secure all that is necessary to perfect the titles of the Connaught proprietors on payment to him of £120,000. The money is paid, but the monarch fails to carry out his part of the agreement. His agent, Wentworth, is recalled, impeached, and expiates his misdeeds on the scaffold. The fight waxes warmer between the king and his subjects; battles are fought and won on either side; the star of Charles wanes at Phlliphaugh: he had been taken prisoner by the Scotch, and for a consideration (£400,000 sterling) was surrendered to the English.

What has old Ireland done during those stirring times across the Channel? Have her arms been palsied by the late seven years' war that culminated in so sad a defeat? Was not her very heart plucked out by confiscations and reverses? Nay, rather, she is quickened into new life; and, on the 23d of October, 1641, the Irish battle-cry rings from one end of the land to the other. The charge comes with the suddenness and effect of an electric storm; and were it not for a Judas in the camp, the most momentous victory ever achieved on Irish soil would have taken place within that twenty-four hours. Despite the treachery, and the loss of Dublin Castle thereby, immense headway was made by the Confederates. They dashed with lightning-like rapidity from place to place, and within a few days were in control of the greater part of the country. A form of government was established, Magna Charta adopted, money coined at the national mint, and the city of Kilkenny became the seat of the Confederation. Envoys returned from France and Spain bearing news of assistance to be rendered, Cardinal Rinuccini came from the Vatican with arms, money, and munitions of war, and Father Luke Wadding forwarded two thousand muskets, four hundred brace pistols, two thousand cartouche-belts, four thousand swords, two thousand pike-heads, and twenty thousand pounds of powder, with matches, shot, and other stores. The money needed to pay for all these articles was contributed in great part by the Irish troops in the service of Spain in the Netherlands. From every month's pay the soldier reserved a stipend, however small, to help in winning back the disenthralment of his native land. Best of all help from abroad was the arrival of Don Eugenius O'Neil, better known as "Eochain Ruadh." He had been a commissioned officer in the Spanish service, and at the call of his country threw up his commission, and came back to fight the old fight again.

For the first time in Irish history there was a fusion of all Anglo-Irish and Irish elements, save of those sundered by religious antagonism. The mind of Europe had not then broadened enough to regard *man* apart from his surroundings and belief; indeed, it has not reached this plane even yet. But an increasing purpose runs through the ages, and nearer and more near comes the day when true manhood will be universally recognized as the standard of the man.—— The fortunes of war, on the whole, favored the Irish army until after the execution of

Charles the First, Jan. 29, 1649. In the month of August following, frenzied with fanaticism, came the brutal and bloodthirsty Cromwell. Whether in England, Scotland, Wales, or Ireland, his career was the same; he killed and slaughtered without remorse, and without mercy, conceiving himself the while, to be a chosen instrument for that purpose. Before he left England a resolution had passed through Parliament confiscating two and half million acres of Irish land to reimburse those who had advanced money to defray the expense of an expedition. This money was mostly expended on the king's troops fighting against the Parliamentary army. Before he left Ireland that country had become a veritable Haceldama, the angel of death had smitten every household, horrors upon horrors, nameless iniquities were perpetrated with fiend-like malignity, six hundred thousand of her children were slain, and Ireland had become worse than a wilderness. From the beginning to the end of this Cromwellian war, says Lord Clarendon, there never was such destruction since the destruction of Jerusalem by Titus. Three millions of pounds sterling were due by the government to the soldiers and to those who had furnished supplies. Immediately a check was drawn for the amount by confiscating eight and a half million acres of Irish land, and to make the check good all the native blood and the old English of the Pale, who were Catholics, should be "transplanted" to Connaught. There is a grim humor in calling these vandal-zealots the champions of freedom of conscience. Any priest found there after twenty days was to be hanged, drawn, and quartered; the same price was set upon his head as upon that of a wolf, and the oath of supremacy required each one to abjure, among other things, "the doctrine which teaches that salvation is to be procured by good works." Framed wisely in good sooth for Cromwell and his Ironsides, for with any other creed salvation of any kind would be theirs not one day sooner than the kalends of Greece.

But an American reader may ask, Is not this England a missionary country? We answer, It is so called; but it has been the sternest and most truculent propagandist of misery and woe to the many-hued peoples of the globe. Over one-third of its surface and one-fifth of its population its sceptre bears sway, its imports and exports are in still larger proportions, and the proud boast is made that the sun never sets on the English dominions. In reaching this towering altitude the cardinal motive in English policy has been the supremacy of England, no matter what barriers interpose, what rights are to be outraged, what injustice is to be done, what sacrifice of life is to be made. France was rent in twain more than once to resist this domineering usurpation; Clive and Warren Hastings, in promotion of such policy, overswept a tract of country from which England in superficial extent might be torn as a tree from the forest. The ports of China were open to the suicidal importation of opium, and Sepoys blown from the mouth of the cannon, to the same obnoxious end. The American Colonies were saved from a like fate by the heroism of their adopted sons, and the chance capture of a random spy. The fading tribes of New Zealand and the now untrodden jungles of Australia bear testimony to the same effect; while, in our own day, the broken assegai of the Zulu, the gallant conduct of the Afghan, and echoes of the Transvaal war multiply proofs of the same truth. They decimate the people and call it order: when these are harried to death by unjust exactions, they call it law.

In the light of these recent events we are disabused of all incredulity as to the savage atrocities of the Cromwellian campaign. Within eleven years as many million acres of land were confiscated in Ireland. And the titles thus acquired were the prevailing ones in Ireland until the " Encumbered Estates Act" went into operation in 1849. A law had been enacted prohibiting those of the Ironsides who received their back pay in land from intermarrying with Irish girls unless they first " conformed " to the religion of the State. The knowledge of the conformation was to be given under oath. The troopers wooed as they fought, but the "nice girl milking her cow"* could not be won over to forswear the religion of her fathers. Each one coaxed her bluff Ironside lover to get married first; and since he abjured the belief that good works were necessary for salvation, he swore afterwards, without scruple of conscience, that she had become a Protestant. In the natural course of events children were born; and since the father, in an isolated country district, had little society other than his wife and children, he developed into *believing* as they believed, and speaking as they spoke, — in the Irish vernacular. This reminds us of meeting American friends of more than the average public school education who were surprised to be informed that there was, nay is, a distinct Irish language, — one running back to the first colonization of the country by the Phœnicians; and in strength, pathos, volume, and melody, little changed to-day from what it was in that elder time. Within the past six months we have seen people melted to tears on listening to an

---

* The name of a well-known Irish song — "Colleen deas crughta na' m-bo."

Irish sermon from a Boston pulpit. It was delivered by a distinguished priest from the West of Ireland. The language is now spoken by less than a sixth of its people.

" 'Tis fading, oh ! 'tis fading, like leaves upon the trees ;
In murmuring tones 'tis dying, like wail upon the breeze ;
'Tis fastly disappearing, like footprints on the shore,
Where the Barrow and the Shannon and Lough Erne's waters roar."

With speaking their own the Irish pretty generally, at that time, spoke also the Latin language. It was just then, too, that an old Irish woman was hanged as a witch on Boston Common for the crime (!) of not being able to repeat the Lord's Prayer in English, though she could, and did, do so perfectly in the Latin. Meanwhile a revolution in sentiment passed over England. Their religious sentiments had been changed four times within an interval of twelve years; their political views assume like chameleon tints. In one case or the other they do not appear to have been mastered by any deepened conviction other than the conviction of self-interest. Cromwell, the glorified barbarian, was exhumed, and hanged at Tyburn. Charles the Second had been recalled, and received with such acclamation that one would think 1649 and its red memories had been blotted out from the pages of English history. The Irish officers and men who fought so valiantly for his father hoped to receive recognition by reinstatement in their possessions. Some small attempt was made to effect this; acts of Parliament were passed, committees appointed, but very little more accomplished. Charles issued a "declaration of indulgence," which was a measure of religious toleration. His Parliament had but scant sympathy with such a spirit, and it was in practice ineffectual. To Charles succeeded his brother, James II. James, in mental stature and breadth of view, no less than in physical courage, was perhaps the ablest of the Stuart dynasty. But his English subjects were stunted in mental growth, and intolerant in opinion. The clash soon came, and he was forced to fly to France. He came to Ireland, and thousands rallied to his standard. Schomberg and his master, William of Orange, followed soon after. The battles of the Boyne and of Aughrim, of Athlone and Limerick, tell the story of victors and vanquished. The story would be incomplete without a confiscation: 1,060,-792 acres of land were confiscated. At the sale, a few years later, an act of Parliament disqualified the Irish from becoming purchasers in fee at the auction, or from buying under lease for a longer period than two years. But the treaty of Limerick, with the manner of its observance, or rather non-observance on the part of the English, is too important to be passed over in a summary way. The legislation enacted thereafter is a key that will unlock many of the puzzles now troubling the public mind, and set at rest doubts honestly entertained as to the necessity of such a movement as the Land League. We may be permitted, therefore, to dwell at some length on the articles of the treaty, as well as on the subsequent legislation. The civil articles run as follows: —

"Between the Right Honorable Sir Charles Porter, Knight, and Thomas Coningsby Esqre Lords Justices of Ireland; and His Excellency the Baron De Ginckle Lieutenant General and Commander in Chief of the English army; on the one part, and the Right Honorable Patrick, Earl of Lucan, Piercy, Viscount Gallmoy, Colonel Nicholas Purcel, Colonel Nicholas Cusack, Sir Toby Butler, Colonel Garrett Dillon, and Col. John Brown; on the other part In the behalf of the Irish inhabitants in the city and county of Limerick, the counties of Clare, Kerry, Cork, Sligo, and Mayo. In consideration of the surrender of the city of Limerick, and other agreements made between the said Lieutenant General Ginckle, the governor of the city of Limerick, and the generals of the Irish army, bearing date with these presents, for the surrender of the city, and submission of the said army: it is agreed, That,

"I. The Roman Catholics of this kingdom shall enjoy such privileges in the exercise of their religion, as are consistent with the laws of Ireland; or as they did enjoy in the reign of King Charles the Second: and their Majesties, as soon as their affairs will permit them to summon a

Parliament in this kingdom, will endeavor to procure the said Roman Catholics such farther security in that particular, as may preserve them from any disturbance upon the account oftheir said religion.

"II. All the inhabitants or residents of Limerick, or any other garrison now in the possession of the Irish, and all officers and soldiers, now in arms, under any commission of King James, or those authorized by him, to grant the same in the several counties of Limerick, Clare, Kerry, Cork, and Mayo, or any of them; and all the commissioned officers in their Majesties quarters, that belong to the Irish regiments, now in being, that are treated with, and who are not prisoners of war, or have taken protection, and who shall return and submit to their Majesties obedience, and their and every of their heirs, shall hold, possess, and enjoy, all and every their estates of freehold and inheritance; and all the rights, titles and interest, privileges and immunities, which they, and every or any of them held, enjoyed, or were rightfully and lawfully entitled to in the reign of King Charles II. or at any time since, by the laws and statutes that were in force in the said reign of King Charles II. and shall be put in possession, by order of the government, of such of them as are in the king's hands, or the hands of his tenants, without being put to any suit or trouble therein, and all such estates shall be freed and discharged from all arrears of crown rents, quit-rents and other public charges, incurred and become due since Michaelmas 1688, to the day of the date hereof: and all persons comprehended in this article, shall have, hold, and enjoy all their goods and chattels, real and personal, to them or any of them belonging, and remaining either in their own hands, or in the hands of any persons whatsoever, in trust for, or for the use of them, or any of them : and all, and every the said persons, of what profession, trade, or calling soever they be, shall and may use, exercise, and practise their respective and several professions, trades and callings, as freely as they did use, exercise, and enjoy the same in the reign of King Charles II., provided that nothing in this article contained be construed to extend to, or restore any forfeiting person now out of the kingdom, except what are hereafter comprised; provided also, that no person whatsoever shall have or enjoy the benefit of this article that shall neglect or refuse to take the oath of allegiance, made by act of Parliament in England in the first year of the reign of their present Majesties, when thereunto required.

"III. All merchants or reputed merchants of

the city of Limerick or of any other garrison now possessed by the Irish, or of any town or place in the counties of Clare or Kerry, who are absent beyond the seas, that have not bore arms since their Majesties declaration in February 1688 shall have the benefit of the second article, in the same manner as if they were present; provided such merchants, and reputed merchants, do repair into this kingdom within the space of eight months from the date hereof.

"IV. The following officers viz. Colonel Simon Lutterel, Captain Rowland White, Maurice Eustace of Yermanstown . . . and others beyond the seas upon affairs of their respective regiments, or the army in general, shall have the benefit and advantage of the second article provided they return hither within the space of eight months, from the date of these presents, and submit to their Majesties Government and take the above mentioned oath.

"V. That all and singular the said persons comprised in the second and third articles shall have a general pardon of all attainders, outlawries, treasons, misprisions of treason, premunires, felonies, trespasses, and other crimes and misdemeanors whatsoever, by them, or any of them committed, since the beginning of the reign of King James the Second; and if any of them are attainted by Parliament, the Lords Justices, and General, will use their best endeavors to get the same repealed by Parliament, and the outlawries to be reversed gratis, all but the writing-clerk's fees.

"VI. And whereas these present wars have drawn on great violence on both parts; and if leave were given to the bringing all sorts of private actions, the animosities would probably continue that have been too long on foot, and the public disturbances last: for the quieting and settling therefore of this kingdom, and avoiding those inconveniences which would be the necessary consequence of the contrary, no person or persons whatsoever, comprised in the foregoing articles, shall be sued, molested, or impleaded at the suit of any party or parties whatsoever, for any trespasses by them committed, or for any arms, horses, money, goods, chattels, merchandizes, or provisions whatsoever by them seized or taken during the time of the war. And no person or persons whatsoever, in the second or third articles comprised, shall be sued, impleaded, or made accountable for the rents, or mesne rents of any lands, tenements, or houses, by him or them received, or enjoyed in this kingdom, since the beginning of the present war, to the day of the date hereof, nor for any waste or trespass by him or them committed in any such lands, tenements, or houses; and it is also agreed that this article shall be mutual and reciprocal on both sides.

"VII. Every nobleman and gentleman comprised in the said second and third articles, shall have liberty to ride with a sword, and case of pistols; and keep a gun in their houses for the defence of the same, or for fowling.

"VIII. The inhabitants and residents in the city of Limerick, and other garrisons, shall be permitted to remove their goods, chattels, and provisions, out of the same, without being viewed and searched, or paying any manner of duties, and shall not be compelled to leave the houses or lodgings they now have, for the space of six weeks next ensuing the date hereof.

"IX. The oath to be administered to such Roman Catholics as submit to the government, shall be the oath above-said and no other — videlicet — I, A. B., do sincerely promise and swear that I will be faithful and bear true allegiance to their Majesties, King William and Queen Mary —So help me God.

"X. No person or persons who shall at any time hereafter break these articles or any of them shall thereby make, or cause any other person or persons to forfeit or lose the benefit of the same.

"XI. The Lords Justices and General do promise to use their utmost endeavors, that all persons comprehended in the above-mentioned articles, shall be protected and defended from all arrests and executions for debt or damage for the space of eight months next ensuing the date hereof.

"XII. Lastly, the Lords Justice and General do undertake that their Majesties will ratify these articles within the space of eight months, or sooner, and use their utmost endeavors that the same shall be ratified and confirmed in Parliament.

"The thirteenth article simply provides for the mode of paying certain money to Colonel John Brown.

"For the true performance hereof we have hereunto set our hands.

"Present:

"S. CRAVENMORE.	CHAS. PORTER.
H. MACCAY.	THOS. CONINGSBY.
T. TALMASH.	BAR. DeGINCKLE.

"And whereas, the said city of Limerick hath been since, in pursuance of the said articles, surrendered unto us: Now Know Ye, that we, having considered of the said articles, are graciously pleased hereby to declare that we do for us, our heirs, and successors, as far as in us lies, *ratify and confirm the same, and every clause, matter, and thing therein contained.* And as to such parts thereof for which an act of Parliament shall be found to be necessary, we shall recommend the same to be made good by Parliament, and shall give our royal assent to any bill or bills that shall be passed by our two houses of Parliament to that purpose. And whereas it appears unto us that it was agreed between the parties to the said articles, that after the words Limerick, Clare, Kerry, Cork, Mayo, or any of them, in the second of the said articles, the words following, viz, 'And all such as are under their protection in the said counties,' should be inserted and be part of the articles. Which words having been casually omitted by the writer, the omission was not discovered till after the said articles were signed, but was taken notice of before the second town was surrendered; and that our said Justices and General, or one of them, did promise that the said clause should be made good, it being in the intention of the capitulation, and inserted in the foul draft thereof. Our further will and pleasure is, and we do hereby ratify and confirm the said omitted words, viz 'And all such as are under their protection in the said counties,' hereby for us, our heirs, and successors, ordaining and declaring that all and every person and persons therein concerned shall and may have, receive, and enjoy the benefit thereof, in such and the same manner, as if the said words had been inserted in their proper place, in the said second article, any omission, defect, or mistake in the said second article, in any wise notwithstanding. Provided always, and our will and pleasure is, that these our letters patents shall be enrolled in our Court of Chancery, in our said kingdom of Ireland, within the space of one year next ensuing. In witness, etc., witness ourself at Westminster the twenty-fourth day of February, anno regni regis, et reginæ Gulielmi et Mariæ quarto per breve de privato sigillo. Nos autem tenorem premissor—predict. Ad requisitionem attornat, general, domini regis, et dominæ reginæ pro regno Hiberniæ. Duximus exemplificand, per presentes. In cujus rei testimonium has literas nostras fieri fecimus patentes. Testibus nobis ipsis apud Westmon quinto die Aprilis, annoque regni corum quarto.

BRIDGES.

" Examinat per nos—

S. KECK,
LACON WM. CHILDE, } *In cancel magistros.*"

The military articles, twenty-nine in number, give all persons, of what quality or condition soever, free liberty to go to any country beyond the seas (England and Scotland excepted) with their families, household stuff, plate, and jewels. " Fifty ships, each of two hundred tons burden, and twenty more if necessary, would be furnished for free transportation. Said ships to be furnished with forage for horse, and all necessary provision to subsist the officers, troops, dragoons, and soldiers, and all other persons wishing to be transported to France, provisions to be paid for on the disembarking at Brest, Nantz, or any other French port. Such part of the garrisons as go beyond seas shall march out with their arms, baggage, drums beating, ball in mouth, match lighted at both ends, and colors flying, with all the provisions and half the ammunition that is in the said garrisons, and join the horse that march to be transported; that the Irish may have liberty to transport nine hundred horses, including horses for the officers, hay and corn to be bought at usual market rates, and General Ginckle will furnish convenient carriages for them to the place where they shall be embarked. All prisoners of war in Ireland on 28th September, to be set at liberty on both sides. Two men of war were to serve as a convoy. That at the signing of the articles the general would send a ship express to France; and besides furnish two small ships to transport two persons to France to give notice of this treaty. The Irish army were also to have six brass guns, two mortar pieces, and half the ammunition in the magazines. There was to be a cessation of arms at land as also at sea, with respect to the ships, English, Dutch, or French, designed for the transportation of the troops. Hostages mutually satisfactory, were to be given for the faithful performance of the articles," which were duly signed.

If honor find no asylum on earth otherwhere, it is sure to find it in the breast of kings, men have said; and every dictate of honor demands the fulfilment of these solemn stipulations. There was a temptation on the part of the Irish to violate them, for three days after signature the promised French fleet cast anchor in Dingle Bay. But Irish honor was pledged, and, happen what might, they would carry out their part of the contract. How was it with England and William? On the 3d of October, 1691, the articles were signed. The English Parliament met on the 22d of the same month, and one of the first acts passed by this body was a partial nullification of the treaty. It had been regarded as the Magna Charta of civil and religious liberty for the Catholics. We see from the first of the civil articles they were guaranteed such privileges in the exercise of their religion as they did enjoy in the reign of Charles the Second, and the Parliament first to meet would procure them such security as would preserve them from any disturbance on account of their said religion. William also promised to obtain a ratification of the treaty from the first Parliament he could convene. That Parliament met, had a fairly long session, and was dissolved without any such measure being submitted. The next Parliament was convened in April, 1695, and in a speech from the throne it was stated that a settlement of Ireland should be made in the Protestant interest.

What was done in pursuance of this declaration? In cap. 4, 7th Wm. III., it was enacted that Catholics should be deprived of the means of educating their children at home or abroad, and should not have the right to act as guardians either of their own children or of the children of others. Next, the Catholics were disarmed. Yet, to indicate that the English felt the binding force and solemn obligation of the treaty, Parliament in 1697 passed an act confirming the articles of Limerick. But it was an emasculated and perfidious confirmation, for there was a complete excision of what gave fibre and backbone to the instrument. The first article was wholly omitted; and omissions and interpolations vitiate the remainder.

We have studiously refrained from more than touching on the religious phase of the controversy. Now we approach a period full of sad interest and instruction on the land question. If we find legislation defining the tenure of the Irish tenant, and marking the limit of the profit which he may recover from his industry; if we find the law encouraging reformers, the spawn of infamy and lepers of decent society in other countries, to look up this amount in Ireland, and if a surplus be found, not only the surplus but the whole, to belong to them as a reward; if we find the principles of morality sapped by laws holding forth incentives to children to rob their parents, to wives to forget their vows, to the community at large to trample on right by fixing an arbitrary price for chattels of a fluctuating value,—then we may infer that legislation is the poison-spring from which misery and unhappiness have flowed. But legislation is void without the seal of the government under a monarchy, and since the first duty of government is the security of life and property,—the welfare of the people,—when it fails in the execution of that trust, still more when it is false to it, it ceases to deserve the name, and becomes misgovernment. When this misgovernment prohibits to four-fifths of the people of a country the common rights of humanity, the use of a church or a school-house—the two great factors in modern civilization—and has laws enacted denying rights that all persons other than criminals should enjoy, then it becomes the parent of injustice, and generates ignorance, poverty, and all the evils that follow in their train. So far as it can, it turns back the hand on the dial of progress, and barbarizes a nation. Having done this, to say that the nation is plunged in sunless depths of ignorance, poverty, and woe by His inevitable decree, is to blaspheme God's providence; to claim that the people are so by their own native depravity, is the flimsiest of transparent shams.

We hold, therefore, that English misgovernment is responsible for the condition of Ireland during three-fourths of the eighteenth century, and that whatever is reprehensible in the surroundings of her people to-day, is a legacy inherited from that time. Had not God implanted a royal spirit in the breast of the race, had he not endowed it with elasticity and a vitality that could not be quenched, with exalted mental gifts and priceless virtue, it would have fallen low as the Helots in Sparta, as the negro race under hard taskmasters, by the profound turpitude of English misgovernment.

As astronomers observe an eclipse to discover the properties of light, let us inquire what was the condition of the people during that time. Their voice was an inarticulate jeremiad: once and again they did break silence, however, when charged with conspiring to help the Pretender; and again, after the middle of the century, to remove imputations cast upon their religion, they published a solemn declaration from which we extract the second, fifth, and seventh sections:

"2d. We abjure, condemn, and detest, as unchristian and impious, the principle that it is lawful to murder, destroy, or anyways injure any person whatsoever, for or under the pretence of being heretics; and we declare solemnly before God, that we believe that no act, in itself unjust, immoral, or wicked, can ever be justified or excused by, or under pretence or color, that it was done either for the good of the Church, or in obedience to any ecclesiastical power whatsoever."

"5th. We do further declare that we do not believe that the Pope of Rome, or any other prince, prelate, state, or potentate hath, or ought to have, any temporal or civil jurisdiction, power, superiority, or pre-eminence, directly or indirectly, within this realm."

"7th. We further declare that we do not believe that any sin whatsoever committed by us can be forgiven at the mere will of any Pope, or of any priest, or of any person or persons whatsoever; but that sincere sorrow for past sins, a firm and sincere resolution, as far as may be in our power, to restore our neighbor's property or character, if we have trespassed on or unjustly injured either; a firm and sincere resolution to avoid future guilt, and to atone to God, are previous and indispensable requisites to establish a well-founded expectation of forgiveness; and that any person who receives absolution without these previous requisites, so far from obtaining thereby any remission of his sins, incurs the additional guilt of violating a sacrament."

Mr. Charles O'Connor, grandfather of our distinguished fellow-citizen, was a member of the committee that drew up this declaration. But this was well on towards the evening. Let us inquire how it fared with the Irish in the dust and heat of the day. As we have seen, the articles were ratified by William and Mary for themselves, their heirs, and successors; yet within a dozen years their whole purpose was lost sight of, and to crimson still more the statute book of England, Anne and the Georges bettered the instructions of William. Under Anne, in 1703, new laws were proposed in direct conflict with the spirit and letter of the treaty. They were referred to a committee of the whole in the Irish House of Commons, after approval in England; and Sir Toby Butler, who had written the articles, was allowed to be heard as counsel for the Irish, in protest against the passage of such laws. He made an admirable speech before the bar of the House, Feb. 22, 1703. He said if the act proposed should pass into a law it would be not only a violation of the articles, but also a manifest breach of the public faith; that it would be the greatest injustice possible for any one people to inflict upon another, and contrary to both the laws of God and man; that the case of the Gibeonites (2 Sam. 21: 1) was a fearful example of breaking the public faith, which, above one hundred years after, brought nothing less than a three years' famine upon the land, and stayed not till the lives of all Saul's family atoned for it; that even among the heathens, and most barbarous of nations all the world over, the public faith had always been held most sacred and binding; that surely it would find no less a regard in that august assembly. He then made a strictly logical argument with its major, minor, and ergo, proving conclusively that the passage of such an act would be a most disreputable and outrageous proceeding. He went through the seventeen sections of the proposed bill, *seriatim,* proving that each was an infringement of one or other of the articles of the treaty. But they would not listen to the voice of the charmer, charm he never so wisely. Next day the bill was engrossed, and sent to the House of Lords. Here a similar protest was made on February 28th, with no different effect; the bill was passed and received the assent of her Majesty on March 4th.

By the third clause, if any son of a Catholic father became a Protestant, the father, owner in fee of the estate, was forbidden to sell, mortgage, or otherwise dispose of it, or to make any provision for his parents, relatives, or other children. The fourth clause debarred him, under a penalty, from acting in the capacity of guardian for his children; a child, however young, pretending to be a Protestant, was taken from his father, and placed in charge of one of another religion. The fifth clause prohibited intermarriages between persons of both religions. By the sixth section those who professed the Catholic religion were declared incapable of purchasing any manors, tenements, hereditaments, or any rents or profits of the same, of holding any lease of lives, or other lease whatever, for any term exceeding thirty-one years. And on this the restriction was imposed, that if the holding produced a profit greater than one-third of the rent reserved, his vested leasehold interest ceased at once, and became the property of the informer who had wriggled himself into the confidence of the tenant. And this class of informers the law declared to be engaged in honorable service for the government.

The English law provided that the eldest son should succeed by inheritance to the fee-simple estate of the father: however, an exceptional act now provided that on the death of a Catholic owner his estate, when there was no real or simulated Protestant heir, should descend, share and share alike, to all his sons; if no sons, to the daughters in like manner; if he had neither sons or daughters, to his collateral kindred,— the obvious motive being to weaken any social importance or political influence that might accrue from the possession of property.

No person could vote at elections without taking the oaths of allegiance and abjuration. Neither could any civil or military position be held without the performance of the same conditions. If a father had " conformed," at his death his Catholic children forfeited the inheritance. If the wife of a Catholic claimed to be a Protestant, the law compelled the husband to give her a separate maintenance and the custody of all the children. The Catholic could neither buy, sell, mortgage, nor inherit real estate; so to say, " could hardly raise his hand without breaking the law." If a Catholic owned a horse worth more than five pounds, on tender of that amount by a Protestant the animal became his, though actually worth from fifty to one hundred pounds. On such tender being made, occasions have arisen when the Catholic shot his own horse, and then told the would-be purchaser he might take the carcass. If a Catholic taught school he was liable to banishment, and if he returned, to be hanged for felony. A Catholic child that attended a Catholic school incurred, when discovered, a forfeiture of all his property. If he went abroad for an education he was liable to suffer the same punishment. A Protestant who married a Catholic lady was subjected to like infamous treatment. To teach the Catholic religion was a felonious offence; to exercise ecclesiastical jurisdiction in the Catholic church was to expose oneself to be transported, and to return therefrom was treasonable, punished by being hanged, disembowelled alive, and afterwards quartered.

Edmund Burke says of this penal code, that it was a machine as well-fitted for the oppression, impoverishment, and degradation of a people, and the debasement in them of human nature itself, as ever proceeded from the perverted ingenuity of man. The people dragged out a wretched existence during this long Arctic night of persecution; remembering happier times intensified its bitterness. Hidden in the glen or mountain cave the priest, with sentries stationed on the crest of the hill, performed the offices of religion, offered up the Holy Sacrifice, and here alone did a ray of hope and consolation shine in on the cloud of despondency that overhung the peasant's lot. The deeps of his nature were touched by the self-devotion of the priest, who carried his life in his hand in order to minister to his spiritual wants. All was not yet lost; for Eternal Justice would vindicate itself in its own good time. We know of the mills that grind slowly. And when pharisaism, selfishness, and inhumanity — and English law was the quintessence of all three — come to judgment before the Nemesis of nations, we believe they will be ground down finer than sifted snow, and form a drastic powder for all the tyrannies on earth.

Dean Swift says, "Rents were squeezed out of the blood and vitals and clothes and dwellings of the tenants, who live worse than English beggars." In one of his papers the Dean, with caustic sarcasm, suggested a new industry to the Irish; that was, preparing and selling babies for human food. Charles Lamb must have had this before his mind when, asked by an elderly matron how he liked children, he stammeringly replied, "B-b-b-boiled, ma'am." The long Arctic night still lingered; but "the fur roughens with the climate;" the Irish ear caught up tones of hope from the past, and listened to whisperings of victory in the future. Come what would, the passion for freedom remained rooted in their hearts, and they would struggle still for a blessing from on high, even though they should wrestle till the morning.

This inflexible devotion of four-fifths of the people of Ireland to the religion of their fathers, to eternal truth as far as they could know it, is a spectacle of supreme significance. They had but to "conform" to the state religion, and abjure their own, and the shackles of slavery would drop from their limbs. They might rejoice in all the honors and dignities of the state. Like the Christians under the pagan emperors, they need but offer the grain of incense, and everything short of the purple would be theirs; yet with a consciousness of doing right they lived on under adverse temporal conditions. Their record in those days may be writ in one word — martyrology.

We have seen how the laws were calculated to pauperize the people. Why should the tenant by rotation of crops, or improved husbandry, render his farm more productive, when, if the profit exceeded one-third the reserved rent, the informer could pounce upon him and eject him from the premises? What was there to stimulate the father of a family in a career of industry, when the profligate son, by conforming, could render the other members of the family paupers, and bring the father's gray hairs in sorrow to the grave? Why should the husband, in season and out of season, moil and toil for his wife and little ones, when the law gave her the power to leave him heart-broken, 'reft of all that he loved, amid the ruin of his prosperity? "*Nil fœdius habet paupertas quam quod homines ridiculos facit,*" writes Juvenal: the worst thing about poverty is that it makes men ridiculous.

The Irish were ground down by the nether millstone, forced by the law to be poor, then ridiculed and taunted with their poverty as a crime. They were mentally impoverished in like manner. The gates of learning were barred against them; and as for their souls, as far as law could do it, for them there was sheer starvation. Mind, body, and soul, bound by a triple chain forged on the anvil of persecution. In process of time the expanding intelligence of the age will have none or little of this iron work: gradually the religious part of the penal double-edged sword is losing edge; but the part regarding agriculture is still keen as ever. The landlords are both makers and administrators of the law, and, in either capacity, do not give even half an eye to any interest but their own. Their tenants, equal to them in all the essentials of humanity, are hardly recognized, certainly not cared for, as human beings. They may make bricks without straw even to the crack of doom, if their future condition is to be gauged by any fellow-feeling of those socially above them.

In the year 1723, so black with the shadow of famine was the country, that the Duke of Grafton, in a speech from the throne, recommended Parliament to pass measures for its relief. And the Primate of the English Church writes, "Since I came here, in the year 1725, there was almost a famine among the poor; last year the dearness of corn was such, that thousands of families quitted their habitations, to seek bread elsewhere, and many hundreds perished." And Arthur Young, regarded by all who take an interest in the subject as most impartial, writes: "But if these exertions of a succession of ignorant legislatures have failed continually in propagating the religion of government, much more have they failed in the great object of natural prosperity. The only considerable manufacture in Ireland, which carries in all parties the appearance of industry, is the linen, and it ought never to be forgotten that this is solely confined to the Protestant parts of the kingdom. The poor Catholics in the south of Ireland spin wool generally; but the purchasers of their labor, and the whole worsted trade, is in the hands of the Quakers of Clonmel, Carrick, and Bandon, etc. The fact is, the professors of that religion [Catholic] are under such discouragements, that they cannot engage in any trade which requires both industry and capital. If they succeed and make a fortune, what are they to do with it? They can neither buy land, nor take a mortgage, nor even fine down the rent of a lease. Where is there a people in the world to be found industrious under such circumstances? It is no superficial view I have taken of this matter in Ireland; and being in Dublin at the time a very trifling part of these laws was agitated in Parliament, I attended the debates with my mind open to conviction, and an auditor for the mere purposes of information. I have conversed on the subject with the most distinguished characters of the kingdom, and I cannot, after all, but declare, that the scope, purport, and aim of the laws of discovery, as executed, are not against the Catholic religion, which increases under them, but against the industry and prosperity of whosoever professes that religion. . . . Those laws have crushed all the industry and wrested most of the property from the Catholics; but the religion triumphs; it is thought to increase. Those who have handed about calculations to prove a decrease, admit on the face of them that it will require four thousand years to make converts of the whole, supposing the work to go on in future, as it has in past time. . . . The system pursued in Ireland has had no other tendency but that of driving out of the kingdom all the personal wealth of the Catholics, and prohibiting their industry within it. The face of the country, — every object, in short, which presents itself to the eye of a traveller, — tells him how effectually this has been done. I urge it not as an argument: the whole kingdom speaks it as a fact. We have seen that this conduct has not converted the people to the religion of government; and instead of adding to the internal security it has endangered it: if therefore it does not add to the national prosperity, for what purpose, but that of private tyranny, could it have been embraced and persisted in? Mistaken ideas of private interest account for the actions of individuals; but what could have influenced the British government to permit a system which must inevitably prevent the island from ever becoming of the importance which nature intended?" This was written in 1778. At the same time Lord Clare said: "It is impossible that any country could continue to exist under a code of laws by which a majority of its inhabitants were cut off from the rights of property."

Meanwhile the country was in a terrible state. In 1741 it passed through a famine during which more lives were lost, it was said, than in the war one hundred years before. The Catholic gentry were emigrating to France, Spain, and the United States. The people had got to the bottom of the box of Pandora, and the last gift itself seemed not to be there. Still stronger, however, than the words of Swift, Lucas, Molyneux, or Berkeley came the muffled voice of a power destined to change the fate of empires. This was the voice of Public Opinion, moulding itself into a thunderbolt to undermine the kingly destinies of France, and to make monarchs tremble on the other thrones of Europe. It was wafted over the waters to Ireland, and that inarticulate jeremiad was forgotten.

But the breeze of liberty that first touched the war-furrowed cheeks of the Green Isle came from America. News of Burgoyne's defeat at Saratoga came across the water. At once, by the 17th and 18th of Geo. III., cap. 49, the most ferocious acts of Anne were rescinded, and the 21st and 22d of the same reign, cap. 24, enlarged the scope of the remedy. By these remedies Catholics might take land on leases for nine hundred and ninety-nine years, or for a term to be determined by a number of lives not exceeding five. They were given the right, too, to devise, bequeath, and convey their estates as fully as others of his Majesty's subjects.

They could also inherit property; and any real or pretended "conformity" of the son would not divest the parent of the estate. They might also purchase or take lands, or any interest in the same, and dispose thereof by will or otherwise. And no longer could his horse be taken from a Catholic on a tender of five pounds. He might now live in Limerick or Galway without being amenable to a penalty; and his goods could no longer be levied on, by a decree of the grand jury, to reimburse those who suffered losses by privateers in time of war. He might even teach school, and act as guardian for his children. Before that defeat petitions had been presented, and fulsome professions of loyalty had been made to the throne by some Tory gentlemen, but the king turned a deaf ear to their petitions and professions; they had merely their labor for their pains. Let us see if they were worthy of their regained liberties.

It was a stirring time in Ireland. Recruiting for the army to fight against the Colonies was fast and furious. Europe blazed like a military volcano, and the United States were in a life or death struggle for independence. The declaration was signed by seven men of Irish birth or descent, in handwriting not indeed so large as that of John Hancock, but to the same effect, staking their lives and their fortunes on the issue. Thus signed Read, McKean, Rutledge, Thornton, Smith, Lynch, and Charles Carroll of Carrollton. And before the " shot heard round the world " was fired, Patrick Henry exclaimed, in the Virginia Convention, "We must fight; I repeat it, we must fight: an appeal to arms and the God of Hosts, that is all we have left." In 1760 Franklin thought the union of the Colonies not only improbable but impossible. "As long as the government is mild and just, as long as there is security for civil and religious interests, the Americans will be respectful and submissive subjects. The waves only rise when the wind blows." The Irish knew the meaning of that mildness and justice; security for civil and religious liberty guaranteed them by treaty they knew the meaning of, too; and now they massed in thousands to the ranks, rocked the cradle of liberty, and by their good swords helped to win the charter of American independence. A brigadier-general of the British army, in his testimony before a committee of the House of Commons after the war, said that General Lee told him " half the rebel Continental army were Irish." The ex-Speaker of the Pennsylvania House of Delegates, Mr. Galloway, reiterated the same statement of his own knowledge. This was the General Lee of whom before and after the battle of Monmouth there was so much ado, many wishing to place him in chief command, others not entirely sure of his sincerity in the cause. Hear what General Howe, who evacuated Boston March 17, 1776, wrote to the home government: " Send out German troops from Europe, for in a war against America and the American people I cannot depend on the Irish people, because a subjugated but unsubdued race are too much in unison — they have too much sympathy for the people of America. The Irish are not to be depended upon." And Arthur Lee, agent of America in Europe, in 1777 wrote to this government: "The resources of our enemy are annihilated in Germany, and their last resort is to the Catholics of Ireland. They have already experienced their unwillingness to go. Every man of a regiment raised there last year obliged them to ship him tied and bound."

It is needless to go fully into this episode; to speak of Washington becoming a member of the Friendly Sons of St. Patrick in Philadelphia, or to tell that in the most crucial time of the whole campaign, when the men were shoeless and with torn uniforms at Valley Forge, this society subscribed the munificent sum of £103,500 sterling of Pennsylvania currency. This was immediately after the reverses at Brandywine and Germantown. Of the committee appointed by Congress to correspond with friends in England, Ireland, and other parts of the world, Silas Deane visited France. Here he made the acquaintance of a man whose history reads like a romance. Pierre Augustin Caron de Beaumarchais was the son of a watchmaker, and was a man of imposing presence and varied accomplishments. He assumed the last name from a small estate owned by his first wife, the widow of M. Francquet. He held a menial office in the Court of Louis the Sixteenth, and by help of Paris Duvernay, the eminent banker, for whom he did some favor, he found means of accumulating a large sum of money in speculation. In thwarting intrigues against the queen, Marie Antoinette, he made himself very popular with the Court. When mutterings of war in the Colonies reached France he was carried away by enthusiasm in their interest. The Minister of Foreign Affairs, M. De Vergennes, was too wary a diplomât to commit himself openly on that side. De Beaumarchais pleaded for them with eloquence, and felt sure of their ultimate triumph. De Vergennes sent him secretly a remittance of a million of livres, and two months later he received the same amount from the king of Spain. A third million was also furnished. With this, it was told him, "you will found a great commercial house, and you will try to draw into it the money of private individuals; the first outlay being now provided, we shall have no further hand in it; the affair would compromise the government too much in the eyes of the English." He established the firm "Roderigue, Hortalez et Cie," he himself the only member. He got together a fleet of forty sail to ply between Bourdeaux and Baltimore, carrying clothing, supplies, and munitions of war for the battalions of the Revolutionary army. The cotton, sugar, and tobacco, to be sent back in return, seldom came. But he kept on in his course without faltering. He had also a man of war, "Le Fier Roderigue," which did good service with D'Estaing in a naval fight off Grenada.

Some insight into his character may be gained by the letter which he wrote on hearing, from the Admiral, of this battle. "Sir, I have to thank you for having forwarded to me the letter from Count D'Estaing. It is very noble in him, at the moment of his triumph, to have thought how very agreeable it would be to me to have a word in his handwriting. I take the liberty of sending you a copy of his short letter, by which I feel honored, good

Frenchman that I am, and at which I rejoice as a devoted adherent of my country against insolent England. The brave Montault [captain] must have thought that he could not better have proved his worthiness for the post with which he was honored than by getting killed; whatever be the result to me, my poor friend Montault has died on the bed of honor, and I feel a sort of boyish joy in the knowledge that those English who cut me up so much in their papers for the last four years will read therein that one of my ships has helped to take from them the most fertile of their possessions. And as for the enemies of M. D'Estaing, and especially of yourself, sir [the minister of marine], I see them biting their nails, and my heart leaps for joy."

This man was nearly always in hot water and called the "French Wilkes." He was the author of "Le Barbier de Seville," and of "Le Mariage de Figaro." Mr. Deane wrote to the secret committee of Congress: "I should never have succeeded in fulfilling my mission here without the indefatigable, intelligent, and generous efforts of M. de

Beaumarchais; the United States are more indebted to him, on every account, than to any other person on this side of the ocean." In the secret proceedings of the First Congress it was also voted that if Spain should declare war against Portugal, the States would fit out privateers to prey on Portuguese commerce.

Louis the Sixteenth had, either from his own funds, or by his security, obtained for the Colonies sixteen millions of livres. A very large contingent of French troops by land and sea had also rendered efficient service; but George W. Parke Custis said, "In the war of the Revolution in this country Ireland furnished one hundred men to any single man furnished by any foreign nation."

Meanwhile, at home, Ireland stood in an erect attitude. The prison door was ajar, and at last the light was breaking. The "volunteers" began to arm in 1776, and the Irish contributed to provide a commissariat. They themselves under the law could not yet bear arms; but the necessity of the times overcame the rigors of the law, and in 1780 fifty thousand Catholics marched with arms in their hands. For nearly two hundred years they were hampered by legal restrictions on trade and commerce; so rigidly so, since the accession of William to the throne, that the recollection of their prosperous trade had almost been obliterated. A distinguished Irishman, called upon to respond to the toast of Irish commerce, said, "I drink no memories." The exportation of cattle from Ireland to England was prohibited. The Irish next sent salted beef and the hides. A new act prohibited this also, declaring it to be a nuisance. The woollen industry kept thousands of hands employed in Ireland, and the raw article was sold at a very high price in the French market. English selfishness, the supremacy of English interests, could not tolerate this transient gleam of prosperity: an act was passed forbidding the exportation of Irish wool to any other country than England, nor would it be received there except by the payment of a heavy duty. The linen industry alone remained; but this was confined to a narrow section of country in the north, and even this suffered from the inveterate jealousy of England. The currency, too, was debased. A patent was given for the manufacture of the smallest coins, for exclusive use in Ireland. George the First was to receive £800 yearly from the patentee, and a certain bonus was to be given to officers of the Crown. This tampering with the currency weakened the confidence between the creditor and debtor classes, and thus impaired the business of the country. The patent, however, proved almost worthless by the strenuous opposition of Swift, who, in the "Drapier letters," partially roused up the slumbering energies of the people. All this time the Catholics were deprived of the franchise; they had no representative in Parliament elected by their votes during the eighteenth century, and were excluded from the Bench, the Bar, the University, — from all civil and military office, — unless they took the oath of abjuration. In 1780 the government was petitioned to abolish all restrictions on Irish trade and commerce. No heed was taken. Meetings were held, and in 1782 the Volunteers, composed indiscriminately of Catholics and Protestants, were massed in Dublin, with their cannon labelled "Free trade for Ireland or —" It was soon after proclaimed that no body other than the King, Lords, and Commons of Ireland had, or of right ought to have, authority to make laws for the Irish people. And thus quasi-local self-government was established. It was not the real article. For at that time Ireland contained a population of from three and a half to four millions. The Catholics were in the proportion of at least six to one, and yet not one of their whole number had a vote. The constitution of the House of Commons too, is a conclusive proof that the country enjoyed no real self-government. Of the three hundred and sixty members of the House only seventy-two were elected by the people; the others represented rotten or pocket boroughs, the nominees of absentee landlords, or rich nabobs at home. Yet, evanescent shadow as it was of the glorious privilege of self-government, Ireland, under its influence, showed wonderful recuperative power, and gave proof that with such a privilege she could stand forth the peer of any nation of equal extent, crowned by the genius of her sons, and the virtue of her daughters.

At Dungannon, in February, 1782, a convention was held by the Volunteers, in which a resolution was passed, almost unanimously, expressing joy at the relaxation of the penal laws against the Catholics. This body was composed of one hundred and forty-three corps of volunteers, all Protestants, and the resolution was the first public manifestation of a feeling that terrified England. With union of sentiment, and one aspiration for their country's welfare, Catholics and Protestants marched shoulder to shoulder, and to their military skill and numerical preponderance, England reluctantly conceded what Grattan, Curran, Flood, Plunkett, and their colleagues could never have attained. In the October of the previous year the " Society of United Irishmen " pledged themselves " to endeavor, by all due means, to procure a complete and radical reform of the people in Parliament, including Irishmen of every religious persuasion." This society included in its membership many of the brightest and ablest men in Ireland. Its paramount object was to effect a *union* between Irishmen of all creeds, and, with this union as a lever, to force England to grant to Ireland all her inalienable rights. It was based on the following principles: 1st. Cordial union among all the people of Ireland in opposition to the English influence in Ireland. 2d. The constitutional means of opposing such influence was declared to be the complete and radical reform of the manner of Parliamentary representation. 3d. No reform to be considered just or adequate which did not include every Irishman of every religious persuasion. The form of initiation was as follows: "I, A. B., in the presence of God, do pledge myself to my country that I will use all my ability and influence in the attainment of an imperial and adequate representation of the Irish nation in Parliament, and as a most absolute and immediate necessity for the chief good of Ireland, I will endeavor as much as lies in my ability, to forward and perpetuate the identity of interests, the union of rights, and the union of power, among Irishmen of all religious persuasions." The founder of the society was Theobald Wolf Tone, and with him were associated Lord Edward Fitzgerald, Napper Tandy, and others, whose names have been handed down as the heritage of freedom.

William Pitt became English minister in 1783, and remained in office until 1801. The efforts made to purify the Irish Parliament were fruitless: motions for Catholic emancipation, and motions for reform, alike, failed; a standing army of fifteen thousand men was brought over, a militia organized, and the Volunteers were disbanded. France was in the throes of the vastest revolution the world has ever seen; her arms set new boundaries to kingdoms and empires, and the United Irishmen, compelled to become a secret organization by the machinations of Pitt, had emissaries passing to and fro between the two countries. Shiploads of arms came to Ireland, and the membership of the society grew enormously large. The First Consul had promised generous co-operation with the prospective attempts of Ireland to recover her rights; but after a personal survey of the French coast, and a careful calculation of his naval resources, Napoleon turned his face to Egypt. Pitt wished nothing better than to precipitate an armed conflict. Spies had informed him of the plans of the leaders. Oliver Bond and his colleague were arrested. There were concentrated, it is estimated, 125,000 troops in Ireland. When the uprising took place England was armed to the teeth, and, in seven months, she strangled with shot and shell seventy thousand of Ireland's best and bravest defenders. Two years after, for pelf and place, the venal legislature sold away the nascent liberties of their country. "Do not unite with us, sir, or we shall rob you," said Dr. Johnson; and so it came to pass. By the Union Ireland's debt was quadrupled in sixteen years, rising from twenty-eight to one hundred and twelve millions of pounds sterling, and the robbery has been going on ever since. We have had no wholesale confiscations, it is true; but the tenants' interests in the soil have been confiscated, year after year, by the rapacious landlords. In the previous century "Whiteboyism" was the only remedy available to enforce fixity of tenure. Whenever the power of public opinion is so moulded as to inspire terror in the wrongdoer; whenever Ireland can fling herself with the skill and discipline of a consolidated phalanx upon England struggling with difficulty; whenever justice and reason have their proper weight in the English Parliament,— then, and only then, can we hope, even in this century, to win back for Ireland what is justly hers. There are barriers to be overcome. Power exercises a fascination over those who control it; and for centuries those who have had the power in Ireland — a small minority of the people — have been the willing tools of the government, and the government has buttressed and fortified their position. There has been an identity of interest between the government and the landlord. If the people cried for bread they gave them a stone; more literally, they gave them a Parliamentary Committee. After the battle of Waterloo, distress and pestilence prevailed in Ireland.

The remedy proposed was clearances of estates. The Parliamentary Committee was appointed, reported what they had seen and heard, recommended legislation as a remedy; but the landlord influence was too strong: nothing was done. Again the wail of famine broke forth in 1822; the government contributed some £300,000, paid for transporting a colony to Peterborough, Canada, as a salve to what it supposed was a conscience; and again the inevitable committee was appointed. Was there any measure proposed to cut out the cancer? Not at all; the landlord influence was still in the ascendant. And in 1826 a bill was passed prohibiting the lessee of land to sublet without the landlord's consent.

In 1829, after the passage of the "Act of Emancipation," another committee was appointed: in 1830, and in 1832, Parliamentary committees were appointed; but the result was invariably the same,—the rights of the landlords were of transcendent importance, and it lay beyond the power of the British Constitution to remedy any abuses arising from the exercise of those rights. And all this time they had before their eyes the example of France, where, from twenty-seven thousand proprietors before the revolution, the number had increased to millions, and in proportion to such increase the country had grown in prosperity; until to-day, with its six millions of proprietors of small holdings, France, in all the resources of wealth and means of advancement, is abreast with the foremost nations of Europe. They knew, too, what had been accomplished by Frederick William of Prussia, under the advice of Stein and Hardenberg. France was a country they had but little affection for, and they may not have cared, however lawful it was, to be taught by an enemy. But Prussia and England fought side by side at Waterloo, and there were pleasant relations subsisting between both countries. In Prussia the landlord could not arbitrarily raise the rent, nor eject his tenant. Yet the cry for reform grew so strong that the king gave the landlords and tenants two years within which to come to a solution of their difficulties. If they failed to do so within the stipulated time, the Crown would assume the responsibility of making a final settlement. And it did so. It gave the landlord a four per cent. interest-bearing bond for the fair value of his estate, and the tenant, through the ordinary channels, paid the government such an amount that in forty-one years both principal and interest were paid in full, and the tenant had become owner in fee of his little estate.

How the ownership of his home develops all the bravery and best qualities of the soldier is abundantly proved by the late Franco-Prussian war, as well as by the late war in the United States, where the armies on both sides fought with a courage and heroism that covered them with imperishable glory. Mindless, however, of such beneficent results the English government still coddles the landlord class, and has done almost nothing for the masses of the Irish people. Two-thirds of the revenue of the country come from the soil; it is, therefore, all-important, even from a fiscal point of view, that the subject would be treated in a liberal, statesman-like manner. It is very plain that it has not had such treatment. William Sharman Crawford, member of Parliament, a distinguished Protestant gentleman, seeing the havoc wrought by the unjust land laws, and the heartless conduct of the landocracy, worked in season and out of season, with might and main, to procure justice for the tenants by a modification of the laws. Twelve times, from 1834 to 1847, he introduced such measures; but as many times owing to the influence of the landlords, — the legislators, — he failed to carry out any measure of relief. Rightly considered, the welfare of the tenant would have been the welfare of the landlord, and an element of strength for the government; but hereditary blindness clouded this prospect, and the tenant still groaned under the yoke of oppression. In the last-named year the sky was overcast with the gloom of famine. That esculent, which was the staple food for three-fourths of the people, the potato, rotted in the ground; the tenants had no margin of reserve funds, — all had gone to pay the rack-rents; the lintels of but few houses were marked with blood, and the angel of death breathed on the face of the people, — fell on the fainting victims in every home. There was weeping and desolation in the land, and yet it was not all barren. Produce, cereals, cattle, were being exported to England, to pay the landlords' rent, — more than enough to feed the starving millions; but the fatal work went on. The people cried out for aid, and those who repeated the cry were called "panic-mongers." The charity of the world was appealed to, and men created in God's image and likeness wept as they met together in all countries of the civilized world to help their brother men in stricken Ireland. Even the stony heart of the paternal (!) government was touched; it saw the fruits of its policy in hecatombs of human beings slain, and whole sections of the country depopulated. At the last hour it was driven to keep step with the charity of the world. Thousands of happy homes were broken up, the holiest ties snapped asunder, and tens of thousands of lives sacrificed. The landlords had previously passed a law by which no man who held more than a quarter of an acre of land could get relief, and this aggravated the distress. The poor-house, at any rate, always repelled the poor man; he had an instinctive dread of entering there. This was based chiefly on his sense of self-respect, and on the love he cherished for his wife and family. For once there they could never, perhaps, meet again; and if they survived the humiliation it would rest as a stigma on the family name. In 1841 the population of Ireland was over eight millions; in 1851, according to the normal rate of increase, it would have been nine millions. When the census commissioners reported, it was found to be 6,552,385; leaving nearly two and a half millions to be accounted for. One-half of these, as well as can be ascertained, had emigrated; the other million and a quarter perished of famine, of fever contracted at home, on board the wretched sailing vessels,—hearses they were called—or brought on by debility resulting from such famine, and ending fatally in Newfoundland.

Would the creation of fee-simple ownership of estates be a shield from such an appalling visitation? God's ways are not our ways; and we may not enter into any scrutiny as to what would take place if his law — reason and justice — were the standard of legislators. But this may be said: that with ownership of his holding, the tenant would have such a strong incentive to labor, such an inspiration to industry, that if an evil day did come, he would have a bank reserve to draw upon, and sufficient security to offer for what he might need from a richer neighbor. England in withholding such a right from the tenant, bowed down by centuries of servitude, has been guilty of a crime that can be atoned for, if at all, only by the most comprehensive measures of reform. John Stuart Mill writes: "Those who think that the land of a country exists for the sake of a few thousand land-owners, and that as long as rents are paid, society and government have fulfilled their function, may see in this consummation [expatriation] a happy end to Irish difficulties. But this is not a time, nor is the human mind now in a condition, in which such insolent pretensions can be maintained. The land of Ireland, the land of every country, belongs to the people of that country. The individuals called land-owners have no right, in morality and justice, to anything but the rent, or compensation for its salable value. With regard to the land itself, the paramount consideration is, by what mode of appropriation and of cultivation it can be made most useful to the collective body of its inhabitants. To the owners of the rent it may be very convenient that the bulk of the inhabitants, despairing of justice in the country where they and their ancestors have lived and suffered, should seek on another continent that property in land which is denied to them at home. But the legislature of the empire ought to regard with other eyes the forced expatriation of millions of people. When the inhabitants of a country quit the country *en masse* because its government will not make it a place fit for them to live in, the government is judged and condemned. There is no necessity for depriving the landlords of one farthing of the pecuniary value of their legal rights; but justice requires that the actual cultivators should be enabled to become in Ireland what they will become in in America, — proprietors of the soil which they cultivate." In the "Fortnightly Review" of last September, Mr. Froude wrote: "The Irish soil, if decently cultivated, would feed twice the population which now inhabits it." And in another place: "England has kept Ireland poor and miserable to prevent the people being troublesome. She destroyed Irish trade and shipping by navigation laws, Irish manufactures by differential duties, and laid disabilities even on its agriculture for fear that the Irish importations should injure the English farmer."

With a full knowledge of these facts "The Irish Tenant League" was established in Dublin in 1850. Representatives were present from each of the four provinces, and it was resolved that there should be a fair valuation of rent between the landlord and the tenant, that the tenant should not be disturbed so long as he paid such rent, and that he should have a right to sell his interest with all its incidents at the highest market value. The next step was to have a parliamentary party to give effect to their policy. The Earl of Derby, who succeeded Lord John Russell as Prime Minister in 1852, resigned the reins of office the same year. On the dissolution, the members of the League worked with a will, and, as far as numbers were concerned, scored a brilliant victory. Forty members were elected professedly in favor of their principles, and in September, 1852, they adopted the following resolution as the chart of future political conduct:—

"*Resolved*, That in the opinion of this conference it is essential to the proper management of this cause that the members of Parliament who have been returned on tenant-right principles should hold themselves perfectly independent of and in opposition to, all governments which do not make it part of their policy, and a Cabinet question, to give to the tenantry of Ireland a measure embodying the principles of Mr. Sharman Crawford's bill."

The Derby ministry was defeated by a majority of nineteen on the 17th of December, and on the 28th of the same month Lord Aberdeen succeeded him. The most verbally uncompromising members of the League forgot all their professions, and took office under the government. The constituents became disheartened, the League lingered on, numbering in its ranks many of Ireland's most cherished patriots, but failing to accomplish anything of permanent value for the tenantry.

At this time public attention was diverted from the difficulties of the tenants to the Crimean war. England and France sent large armies to help "The sick man of Europe" against Russian aggression. Later on reinforcements came, also, from Sardinia, the battles of Alma and the Inkerman had not yet been fought, and men who believed that England's difficulty was Ireland's opportunity looked forward to see something done. But Ireland's strength had been shrivelled by the dread ordeal through which it had passed, many of her leaders were no more, others were leagues and leagues away from her shores, and the war came to an end.

These same men, who keep up the long vigil for liberty, are now watching with keen interest the march of events in Central Asia. They see the Russian outposts well on to Candahar, and they regard it a question less of years than of months to see Russia and England locked in deadly combat for the largest jewel in the crown of the empire. When that conflict comes between the Bull and the Bear it would not be strange, if concessions now demanded are not made, to see the Irish matador leap into the arena and striking the bovine animal, a tergo, leave him snorting in the dust. Not a professional way to strike, you say. War is not a school in which instruction is given in what is equitable.

The Crimean war impressed upon Russia the lesson of the necessity of reform. It had floated down the stream for nearly two centuries in a state of half-barbaric splendor, and was looked upon by the inhabitants of other countries in Europe as the embodiment of all that was despotic and tyrannical. After the death of the Emperor Nicholas, his son, Alexander II., took steps to abolish serfdom in his dominions. A committee was appointed in 1857, the collective wisdom of the nation was enlisted in the work, and, in 1861, twenty-three millions of serfs were emancipated. And not only was that done: they were established as proprietors of the soil they cultivated. This soil embraced three hundred millions of acres, and the government — Alexander the Second — indemnified the one hundred and ten thousand owners for their vested rights, by the payment of one hundred millions of pounds sterling. In the discussions before emancipation, some Russians favored placing the serfs in the same position as tenants in Ireland; but this idea was abandoned because of the "abject misery and semi-barbarism" of such a state. In its internal administration, its civil and military development, and its material progress, Russia has made wonderful advancement; so that, with liberal ecclesiastical, civil, and political reform, a country hardly licked into shape at the beginning, will have grown to symmetrical greatness before the end, of this century.

Now what is this abject misery, this semi-barbarism of the Irish tenant, which the English law has encouraged for nearly three centuries? Speaking of the owners of estates in Ireland, John Bright says: "The proprietors of land in Ireland are few in number for a country so large, and among them are those who hold estates, properties which, or a part of which, they can let, — I mean estates of eighty or one hundred acres. Over that, I suppose, there are not more than 12,000, or 14,000 owners in Ireland. One-third of Ireland is possessed by 292 persons; one-half of Ireland is possessed by 744 persons; and two-thirds of the whole island are in the possession of 1,942 persons. But on the other hand, there are more than 500,000 tenants. There is a great fact, — 500,000 families, having at least from two and a half to three millions of persons dependent upon the soil, competing with each other for the possession of a farm; having no variety of occupations as there is in England; having, of course, only one way, and that only the way out of the country, to escape from the difficulties in which they find themselves. These 500,000 tenants are living, as they allege, for the most part in a condition of continual insecurity. . . . The farmers are, in the main, industrious and honest. There has been no country in Europe, no part of the United Kingdom, in which rents have been more generally and constantly and fairly paid than in Ireland, until the recent troubles."

In 1870 the total number of agricultural holdings in Ireland was ascertained to be 608,864, and the rural population 4,286,019. Now let us examine the nature of the occupancy, and the manner in which landlords treat those who occupy the holdings. No better example, perhaps, could be given of the truth of the maxim "*consuetudo legis habet vigorem:*" custom has the force of law, — than the existence of what is known as the "Ulster custom." In the northern province of Ireland this custom has been in operation for two hundred and fifty years. We have seen what was done by James the First to root the colonists in the soil, and this custom was an outgrowth of that policy. In brief, it guarantees to the tenant continuous occupancy while he pays his rent, and that the rent would not be raised by reason of any improvements made by him. Furthermore, that he would have, so to say, a joint interest with the landlord in the soil, and he could dispose of this interest, often more valuable than the fee-simple, irrespective of the wishes of the landlord. To the existence and enforcement of this custom may be attributed, very largely, the exceptional prosperity of Ulster. Of late years the custom has been infringed on very seriously, and the tenants there, now, are at one with their brothers in the other provinces to ameliorate their condition. If the times were uniformly good, the custom would work admirably in the tenant's interest; but when a series of bad seasons follow one another, the tenant, if able to pay his rent, cannot sell his good-will for anything like the amount expended in improvements. One would think that so equitable a provision would be incorporated in the law for the whole kingdom; the landlord influence has been too strong, therefore it was never done. In Leinster, where there is some of the richest pasturing land in the world, the tenants commonly occupy under long leases. But in the western and southern provinces, Connaught and Munster, the occupants are mostly tenants at will, and are kept down by the iron hand of the landlords in a condition of "abject misery and semi-barbarism." They are the worst-housed, worst-clothed and worst-fed peasantry of Europe, and all because of the conditions of the tenancy sanctioned and enforced by English law. The rents are excessive, frequently fixed by competition. Why, it may be asked, does the tenant compete for a holding, or pay excessive rents? The reason is, that there is no other avenue open to him; to climb the hill of comfort, even to gain the means of existence, there is practically but one path, and that is, possession of a holding of land. His wife and children must be provided for. Next to the Supreme Being he loves them and his native land, and to translate this love into act he is willing to do anything but the impossible. The tillage is inadequate to support his family and pay the rack-rent; and he passes over to Scotland or to England to earn enough, at harvest-time, to meet the demands of the landlord. The wife helps him in the fields; the children are kept from school to render the place more productive; if he has laid by any money he spends it all in improvements on the house, or in reclaiming waste land, and next year the place looks so much better, that an increased rent is put upon the holding. The same process is repeated the ensuing year. The third year, by climatic changes or other causes, the crops fail; with all his efforts it is impossible to pay the rent; he is served with a notice to quit, and sent adrift on the world without one cent in compensation for the outlay and improvements he had made. Rent is paid at the expiration of every six months, and it is not uncommon for landlords on "gale" day to serve the tenant with a notice to quit; not actually intending to put it in execution, but providing for contingencies so that, if necessary, no time would be lost in having him evicted from the premises. We can easily imagine the sense of trepidation and unrest under which the tenant labors while this sword of Damocles hangs over the fortunes of himself and his family. Yet such is the form of tenure under which seventy-five per cent. of the tenant farmers of Ireland exist, and such is the method of treatment they receive from the landlords. Is there no remedy for this colossal wrong; no just way of putting an end to a system so pernicious? Mr. Gladstone supposed there was, and tried in 1870 to effect a reform. But he simply tried to lop off the branches, and did not put the axe to the root of this upas-tree.

The chief provisions of the Irish Land Act of that year were as follows:

1st. To give legal recognition to local customs, such as the Ulster custom, and to enforce them against the landlord. The customs, however, were not defined.

2d. It recognized the fact that capricious evictions were of frequent occurrence, by granting to the tenant "disturbed in his holding by the act of the landlord," a maximum compensation of two hundred and fifty pounds sterling.

3d. It encouraged the tenant to invest his money in the farm by giving him, unless he had sold his interest, "a compensation to be paid by the landlord in respect of all improvements on his holding made by him, or his predecessors in title." This compensation for disturbance or improvements was compulsory in all cases where the government valuation of holdings was under fifty pounds; tenants paying rent on a higher valuation might disqualify themselves by contract from the benefit of the act.

4th. To discourage arbitrary raisings of rent, it allowed tenants who paid an annual rent not exceeding £15, to claim for disturbance of tenancy on refusal to pay an increased and exorbitant rent, " if the court shall certify that the non-payment of rent causing the eviction has arisen from the rent being an exorbitant rent." The court might disallow the claim of the tenant if he refused reasonable terms of continuing his tenancy.

5th. It gave facilities for converting tenants into owners in fee-simple, by providing that the tenant should get from the government, when he purchased by agreement, two-thirds of the purchase money, to be repaid, principal and interest, in thirty-five annual payments.

The above third and fourth clauses are what are called "The Bright clauses of the Land Act." Perhaps it would be a sufficient commentary on the inadequacy of the act to state that during the ten years that have elapsed since its passage, not less than twenty-eight bills have been introduced into Parliament for its amendment. The avaricious spirit of the rapacious landlords was outraged by such an act, and at once they began devising schemes to neutralize the good it meant to do, if not to render it a dead letter. The highest legal talent was employed to secure this object. The following letter, written by the Very Reverend President of Maynooth College, is conclusive evidence on this point.

Writing to the "Freeman's Journal" he says: "1st. My evidence regarded chiefly, I may say almost exclusively, the case of this college and the eviction of its Trustees from their college farm of Laraghbryan, as an illustration of the peculiar view of landlord rights held by His Grace the present

Duke of Leinster. The trustees of Maynooth — that is to say, the four archbishops and twelve of the bishops of Ireland — were evicted from their holding because, though consenting under compulsion to pay the increased rent demanded, they would not sign the form of agreement unhappily known as the 'Leinster' lease. I need not burden your columns with a detailed statement of the ingenious devices embodied in this document for practically abrogating, so far as it was possible for legal ingenuity to do so, the provisions, inadequate as they were, of the Land Act of 1870; but I think it right to state that I hold in my possession a letter from His Grace's agent to the secretary of the Maynooth trustees, in which the agent expresses his opinion that there must be 'some misapprehension on the part of the trustees as to the terms of the lease,' inasmuch as it was a strictly legal document, and had, in fact, been drawn by two Queen's counsel expressly 'to meet the provisions of the Land Act of 1870.' In my evidence, it is necessary to add, I brought this noteworthy statement under the consideration of the commissioners. I trust the disclosure of it may lead the Ministry, who are now responsible for the government of this country, to see that it is a hopeless task to attempt to meet the difficulties of the great crisis that is before them if they confine themselves to the framing of a Land Act, the provisions of which can be 'met,' that is to say, evaded and neutralized, by the ingenuity of counsel, however learned in the law. 2d. In the second place I feel called upon to put before the commissioners, as also illustrated by the dealings in connection with the Leinster lease, another main source of the now admitted failure of the Land Act of 1870. The act went upon the supposition that tenants of holdings valued above £50 a year enjoy 'freedom of contract,' and should therefore be left without legal protection. There is an obvious fallacy in this. 'Freedom of contract,' no doubt, exists to this extent — that the persons in question are rational beings, with full liberty of action, and, it may be conceded, notwithstanding the difficulties of their position, in the undisturbed possession of their faculties, so that they fully comprehend the nature of the contract into which they are called upon to enter. But in any other sense 'freedom of contract' is for them an empty name. The possession of a farm may be for such a tenant the *sine qua non* of decent subsistence. It may even be his only means of livelihood outside the walls of a workhouse. But on the Duke of Leinster's estate of 68,000 acres he cannot obtain a farm of any size, however small, at any rent, however exorbitant, without signing the 'Leinster' lease. Is it any wonder that an act should to so large an extent have broken down, which went upon the theory that in such cases freedom of contract existed in any sense worthy of the name? Our trustees exercised their 'freedom' by steadfastly refusing, as in the interest of the tenant farmers of Ireland they were surely bound to refuse, to sanction by their signature the 'Leinster' lease. The result was eviction. Let us hope that the official statement of this transaction, which will soon be placed before Parliament in the report of the commission, will have the effect of convincing the Legislature that a 'freedom of contract' which can be exercised only under a penalty that for a tenant farmer means absolute ruin, is not again to be relied upon as a plea for the insertion in a land act of clauses enabling any landlord in Ireland to coerce his tenants into a forfeiture of the rights to which Parliament considers them entitled." . . . Freedom of contract for the tenant farmer in Ireland has been a mere name. The land he must have on any terms, and the landlord is free to accept or reject his proposal. It is a one-sided freedom, and contracts so entered into cannot be said to have much binding obligation. Again, in all the valuations of the land up to 1870, the landlords had been receiving yearly compensation for the confiscated improvements of evicted tenants.

What is meant by this word "eviction" that we meet with so often? It is a word, alas! of doleful sound, and has been the death-knell of thousands in and out of Ireland.

"See him in his cabin rude,
　Or dancing with his dark-eyed Mary,
You'd swear they knew no other mood
　Than mirth and love in Tipperary."

But all this mirth is ended, and replaced by the sadness of despair when the crowbar brigade moves down on the village in Tipperary. Rude as was the cabin it sheltered all that were dear to the peasant; of all places on earth it was the one spot hallowed in his thoughts, smiling with the joy of his wife, lit by the love of his children. The green hills, the primrose bank, the budding hawthorn tree, framed a picture that could never be effaced from his memory. It was consecrated, too, as the home of his forefathers for generations. When the evil day came, and the exorbitant rent could no longer be paid — even the act of 1870 gave no compensation for disturbance or improvement in case of eviction for non-payment of rent — then he was ruthlessly driven from his dwelling, and left an outcast on the road-side. If he could not scrape together enough of money to emigrate, the poor-house stared him in the face.

The following letter is from the pen of an eye-witness of such a scene: —

"Carna, Connemara, Feb. 15, 1881.

" *To the Editor of the Freeman:*

" Dear Sir, — It is with a sick and aching heart that I disclose the facts I witnessed yesterday, when called on to impart the last rites of religion to a man and wife prostrate in a bed of sickness. It was a sickening and painful sight: — badly clad parents, brought to this pass by impossible rents; famishing children, saved from death by the Mansion House Fund last year, turned out under the cold and rain of yesterday, their potatoes and their chattels scattered on the street; the sorrowing cries of the mothers, the tears and sobs of the innocent children, and the unpitying resolve of an attendant, who fastened the doors behind them, are sights that would make angels weep in sympathy, and cause the most unbending government, even at the eleventh stage of its Protection Bill, to pause and reflect before putting this murderous weapon in the hand of the selfish hacks of the rent offices. When the houses were closed came the most painful scene of all. A feeble old woman, who, owing to her age and debility, was unable to be removed, fainted in the arms of three stalwart constables. So great was the shock she received that her life was despaired of. I fear it will be the real sentence of death for the poor woman. Her husband is unconscious on his bed of sickness for the last three years. He was attended by the parish priest and doctor yesterday. Yet he, too, must go out. The law is absolute and mandatory, and must be obeyed, even at the risk of his life. It was only when the doctor interposed, stating that he was totally unfit to be removed to hospital, and that they would be responsible for his life, that the constabulary, who discharged their painful duty throughout with sense and moderation, paused to consult further orders. It is stated they will return to-day. It is high time for a Liberal government to step in and protect the lives of the people from the fell system which is driving peaceful subjects to desperation and the country to ruin. How long will the fountain of justice remain poisoned in our case?

"I am, dear sir, faithfully yours,
"Patrick Colgan, C. C."

Between 1841 and 1861 there were 270,000 such scenes witnessed in Ireland, representing 1,300,000 souls. Think of the grief and agony of this vast multitude; the remorseless agency of the law carrying out the mandates of vampire landlords, — a law which they themselves helped to enact, — and then say, if you can, there is no necessity for the Land League. For the same agency is still at work. During the first six months of 1880, 1,696 heads of families were evicted. Some were put back as care-takers, we are told. The meaning of this is, that as a sop to outraged public opinion, the landlord gave temporary shelter to the evicted tenant. But he retained the right, under the law, at one week's notice, to bring such care-taker before any petty magistrate, and have him summarily ejected. There are 320,000 holdings in Ireland valued under eight pounds a year, and of these, 175,000 are valued under four pounds a year. Now, the landlords, desiring to get rid of any number of these tenants, bring writs of ejectment to the quarter sessions. To effect the same end more expeditiously, they bring, at times, Dublin writs, and the tenant must pay the costs,—thirty shillings costs for a holding of four pounds valuation. When Dublin writs are brought the costs not infrequently vary from twenty to one hundred pounds,—sometimes more than the entire year's rent. But the valuation of the estate, though based on improvements made by the tenant, is by no means the measure of the rent. Rents are generally double, sometimes treble, nay, quadruple the valuation. And, meanwhile, the price of all cereals, by foreign competition, has been reduced fifty per cent., so that the task of the Irish tenant has been the old story of Sisyphus over again, scratched with briers and thorns in rolling the stone up the mountain, only to begin the struggle anew when he had once reached the top. And this profitless task is imposed upon him by the wicked legislation of England.

We have seen, by the chief provisions of the Land Act of 1870, that it failed to provide for the exigencies of the case. Finding it ineffectual, the Irish members of Parliament, under the lead of Isaac Butt, presented another bill. This was said to involve two, at least, of the three F. F. F.'s — fixity of tenure and fair rents. The bill consisted of ninety clauses, all drawn with the skill and acumen for which Mr. Butt was so remarkable, but clauses that were remedial for the tenant presupposed his financial ability to cope with the landlord in a court of law. For these and more fundamental reasons, the bill met with but little favor among his brother members. Some of the number grew restive and chafed under his leadership; but the welfare of Ireland had been the pole-star of his life. Though beginning his public career as a Tory, he was called, out of the abundance of his heart, to the patriotic ranks, and since then had never faltered in his devotion to their principles. For all that was lofty and ennobling in his past, they bore with him, until, in the early part of 1879, his voice was hushed forever, — he had passed over to the majority.

But the Ireland of other days, in the character of its children, was now undergoing a transformation. The underlying root of all their troubles, the system of land-tenure, still marred all their efforts to better their condition. A radical change was vital, not only to their improvement, but even to their existence. It was talked over, and pages and pages written on the subject. The life-blood of the people was being drained away to pay an inequitable rent, and the harvest did not respond to the labors of the spring-time. In 1877–78, and the two succeeding years, Ireland suffered in a greatly reduced yield of its staple productions. What little had been treasured up for a rainy day vanished. A banker in one county, who held ten thousand pounds of tenant farmers' funds, said that he had paid them nine thousand to meet existing wants. American produce lessened the prices of articles of consumption, and depression of trade in England had the same tendency. The yield of oats, wheat, barley, rye, of hay, of turf was grievously small; some had rotted in the ground from excessive moisture, and a blight fell upon the potato. With a forecast worthy of all praise, the men in Ireland saw the chronic result of the land system — the gaunt spectre of famine — approaching in the distance. It was no visitation of God to wreak vengeance on his people, for there are no braver, more honest, hospitable, kind-hearted, or purer people on the face of the earth than the Irish. Mr. Cowen, in the British Parliament, said last month: "In other countries, and in our own self-governed colonies, Irish legislators are not tabooed. A few years ago, by a singular coincidence, three of the leading powers of Europe had in offices of the highest responsibility, descendants of old Irish exiles. At the same time three of our colonies had in posts of equal authority, three other Irishmen, whom we had banished as rebels in 1848. If Irishmen can rule with success in Australia and Canada, if we can entrust them with the direction of hazardous campaigns in Afghanistan and South Africa, surely we may trust them to assist in administering their own affairs at home. Until we do this, all our efforts to pacify Ireland will fail, — fail egregiously, and, I may add, deservedly."

This says enough for their ability. For their industry at home, see the writings of Arthur Young, of Wakefield, and McCullough; and abroad, "*Quæ regio terræ nostri non plena laboris?*" — what country on earth is there not full of the monuments of our industry? Looking down the dark vista, the leaders, in the spring of 1879, saw that the drama of 1847 was to be re-enacted, if prompt measures were not taken to prevent it. The landlords demanded that the tenants should adhere to the letter of the bond. What though the children starve, provided they get the rack-rent; let the tenant live in squalor and wretchedness, if only he gives them wherewithal to live in extravagance and dissipation. So it had been before, so would it *not* be now; for a new doctrine, one based on true principles of political economy, is preached to them. The tenant should not see his wife perish of hunger, nor see his children starve by any suicidal act of his, in paying money over to the landlord to which he was not rightfully and equitably entitled.

Under the Roman law, whenever a season of distress came on, the tenant had a suspension or entire abatement of the rent, and this is consonant with true principles of equity. Education has made a great change in the character of the people. There are over a million of children in attendance at the national schools now, and the generation just grown to manhood had all the mental attributes required to weigh well the force of the arguments presented by the leaders in the new agitation. In the stress of the bad times petitions were made to the landlords for a reduction in the rents, but the landlords, superciliously, laughed them to scorn. The pulse of the nation was stirred as it seldom had been before, the atmosphere was charged with a spirit that would no longer brook the commission of injustice. The alarm of famine was given, but the landlord still urged his claims. The people, however, wished to keep within constitutional lines, and in mapping out the plan of the campaign it was decided that public meetings should be held all over the country.

At the outset the struggle was confined to Mayo, the second largest county in Connaught. The first public meeting was held in April, 1879, at Irishtown, a small place some few miles distant from Claremorris. Mounted men with green sashes, American flags, and banners with all manner of strange devices, delegations to the number of twenty thousand men, accompanied by bands of music, — such was the brilliant opening of a movement that has attracted the attention of the civilized world. This was the preamble to the resolutions: "From the China towers of Pekin to the round towers of Ireland, from the cabins of Connemara to the kraals of Kaffirland, from the wattled homes of the isles of Polynesia to the wigwams of North America, the cry is, Down with the invader, down with the tyrants. Every man must have his own land, every man must own his home." The chairman of the meeting stated that, since the 1st of January up to that time, three hundred and fifty tenants had been evicted. Then he closed his speech in the following words: " Those who take the lands of evicted tenants are enemies of the country, and as culpable as the landlords." Mr. Brennan said, " I believe it is not on the floor of the English House of Commons, but on Irish soil that the real struggle for independence must be fought." Other speakers followed in the same key, and the meeting closed amid unbounded enthusiasm. The next monster meeting, with similar accessories, was held at Westport, in the same county; and here two of the speakers were men whose names are household words all over Christendom today, — one, the owner of a large estate, bordering on a spot whose beauty is set in the amber of the sweetest of Moore's melodies; the other, the occupant of a prison cell, which he entered with a heroism not less than that of him who entered the camp of Lars Porsena; both brothers in heart, animated by one purpose, and having only one rivalry — to see who, within the limits of law and order, can do the most for the regeneration of his native land. Michael Davitt spoke to the following resolution:

"That whereas all political power comes from the people, and that the people of Ireland have never ceased to proclaim their right to autonomy, we hereby re-assert the right of our country to self-government."

Mr. Davitt, in his usual earnest and forcible way, addressed the people, saying that they had an inalienable right to the possession of the soil; that it was unrighteously taken away; and that they should not accept any settlement of the question as final or satisfactory until the land was given back to those who cultivate and improve it. Charles Stewart Parnell spoke to a resolution requiring a readjustment of the land tenure "on the principle that the occupier of the land shall be the owner thereof." In that speech he first made use of the phrase that has now become historic: "Hold a firm grip of your homesteads." The meeting was a pronounced success. The next great meeting was held in Milltown, in the county of Galway. After this, on July 13, a monster meeting was held at Claremorris. Up to this time members of the hierarchy had fought shy of the movement, but all misapprehension was then explained away, and they have been powerful auxiliaries in the movement ever since. Mr. Parnell next addressed an immense gathering of the people at Limerick. The spark enkindled at Irishtown fanned into a blaze the torpid energies of the race, and it was determined to go on, without let or stay, in the crusade against tyranny and oppression. In August of the same year, a meeting was held at Castlebar; here an organization was formed, and "The National Land League of Mayo" elected its officers. Mr. Louden was elected president, Mr. Daly vice-president, and this was the formal inception of the Land League movement. Meetings continued to be held, and it was found that to meet the wishes of the people in every province, a national organization should be formed. In pursuance of such wishes a call for a convention was issued, and, in October, the following gentlemen were elected executive officers of the "National Land League of Ireland": President—Charles Stewart Parnell, M. P.; Treasurers—Patrick Egan, Joseph G. Biggar, M. P., and W. H. O'Sullivan, M. P.; Honorary Secretaries—A. J. Kettle, Michael Davitt, and Thomas Brennan. The following are the objects of the National Land League of Ireland: —

The National Land League of Ireland was formed for the following objects:

First. To put an end to rack-renting, eviction, and landlord oppression.

Second. To effect such a radical change in the land system of Ireland as will put it in the power of every Irish farmer to become the owner, on fair terms, of the land he tills.

The Means Proposed to effect these Objects are:

First. Organization amongst the people and tenant farmers for purposes of self-defence, and inculcating the absolute necessity of their refusing to take any farm from which another may be evicted, or from purchasing any cattle or goods which may be seized upon for the non-payment of impossible rent.

Second. The cultivation of public opinion by persistent exposure in the press and by public meetings of the monstrous injustice of the present system and of its ruinous results.

Third. A resolute demand for the reduction of the excessive rents which have reduced the Irish people to a state of starvation.

Fourth. Temperate but firm resistance to oppression and injustice.

How the Land League of Ireland Expects its Supporters in America to Aid it.

Irishmen in America can give most effectual aid,

First. By enlightening American public opinion as to the working of the landlord system, and by exposing, through the columns of the American press, the oppressions and outrages which are practised on the tenant farmers of Ireland.

Second. By the immense moral influence which their support exerts on the people at home, encouraging them to be steadfast in the struggle, and not to give way to despair.

Third. By contributing sufficient money to enable the League to carry on the movement in Ireland on a scale such as is necessary to insure success.

Purposes for which Financial Assistance is Asked from America.

Up to the present, through want of money, the League has been obliged to confine its operations chiefly to a few counties. The purposes for which funds are needed are:

First. To enable the League to spread its organization throughout the thirty-two counties of Ireland.

Second. Pending the abolition of landlordism, to aid local branches of the Land League to defend in the courts such farmers as may be served with processes of ejectment, and thus enable them to obstruct such landlords as avail themselves of the poverty of the tenantry and the machinery of the law to exterminate the victims of the existing system.

Third. To enable the League to afford protection to those who are unjustly evicted.

Already the League has been obliged to undertake the support of the families of the men who were recently sentenced to imprisonment for resisting eviction in one of the famine districts, and is now supporting evicted families.

Fourth. To oppose the supporters of landlordism whenever and wherever they endeavor to obtain any representative position in Ireland which would be the means of aiding them in prolonging the existence of the present land laws.

Meanwhile, the government had become awed at the proportions the movement assumed, and, resorting to its old strategy, sought to suppress it. With this intent it arrested for sedition, and lodged in jail, Mr. Davitt, Mr. Daly, Mr. Brennan, and Mr. Killeen. The people, not at all alarmed at this proceeding,—indeed, some such step had been looked forward to,—still kept on in their crusade for tenant emancipation. A preliminary hearing took place at Sligo, the accused were remanded, never brought before a jury, the Beaconsfield ministry having failed to secure sufficient evidence for conviction. But now the cry of famine sweeps over the west and south of the country. It is echoed, too, in the mountains of Donegal, and but faintly heard in the province of Leinster. The potato crop is less in value by ten millions of pounds sterling than the average yield, and this disaster, coming after two successive bad seasons, fills the minds of the people with fear, shrouds the face of the country in a veil of despair. The English government pooh-poohed the existence of famine; but in the middle of December the Duchess of Marlborough, swayed by the noblest feelings, true to her instincts of womanhood, writes a letter to the "Times," proclaiming the magnitude of the distress, and the urgency of the demand for relief. All that is divine in man is imaged in the well of charity; this well is fed by a thousand streams, and they now began to flow in the direction of Ireland. "The Duchess of Marlborough's committee," and "The Mansion House committee," to help the poor Irish peasant, the victim of nefarious laws, received contributions from Australia, from Madras, Bengal, Hyderabad, Candahar, South Africa, Tasmania, New Zealand, from Demerara, Buenos Ayres, Canada, Newfoundland, France, England, Scotland, Wales, and the United States. The United States government fitted out the frigate " Constellation," part of the cargo was furnished by the present mayor of New York city, and the gifts of the other donors he got on board free of all expense. In Paris, a "*Comité de secours aux Irlandais*" was immediately formed, headed by the Cardinal Archbishop, and 700,000 francs were contributed. From Melbourne came £62,735, making, altogether, from Australia proper, Tasmania, and New Zealand, £95,000; summing up a grand total, to the Mansion House fund, of £180,000; to the Duchess of Marlborough's relief fund, of £135,000, including Queen Victoria's contribution of one day's pay.

The Relief of Distress (Ireland) Act, 1880, and its amendment, sanctioned the giving of a loan to the amount of a million and a half of pounds sterling, to the commissioners of public works in Ireland, to sanitary authorities, and to grand juries, in order to aid in the relief. In the distressed districts the total amount applied for was £1,209,852, and the amount sanctioned, £1,139,374. The "Seed Supply Act," in like manner, gave boards of guardians authority to provide seed potatoes, seed oats, and other seed, for occupiers of small holdings, the seed to be paid for by two convenient instalments; and over half a million was obtained for this purpose.

But the United States not only sent money to the "Mansion House Committee," and fitted out the "Constellation"; it also gave a magnificent reception and a large amount of money for the famine fund, to Charles Stewart Parnell. Members of the Land League were first to hoist the signal of distress for the people; its intensity was so great, so overwhelming in the west and south, and in parts of Ulster, that even refusal to pay rents, and holding a fast grip on their homesteads were inadequate to keep back the wolf of famine from the doors of the tenantry. The air was laden with the unspoken wants of the people, and Mr. Parnell, accompanied by his friend Mr. Dillon, hastened to the United States. If he had not retained a vivid recollection of the nature of his mission, it would have been a triumphant ovation. He was received by the highest dignitaries wherever he went,— by State legislatures, and by the House of Representatives at Washington, in a manner to prove, beyond all controversy, the depth and extent of the sympathy felt for Ireland in this country. He travelled over sixteen thousand miles, visited sixty-two cities, and received for relief of the distress forty-eight thousand pounds. This was distributed, without incurring any expense, by the Central Committee of the Land League, and the subordinate branches in Ireland. In January, 1880, he visited Boston, and before an immense meeting in Music Hall, delivered the following address:—

LADIES AND GENTLEMEN,—As our worthy president has truly said, while you in this country give help to Ireland to meet the present emergency, you also, I feel sure, after having investigated the causes which brought about that necessity, bestow upon us your sympathy and assistance in removing those causes. From time to time Ireland has been in the position of being compelled to come before the nations of the world as a mendicant. We have a fertile soil, a good climate, and an industrious people; and yet every ten or twenty years famine sweeps our land, and we are obliged to appeal to the charity of you and of others to keep our people from starvation. It has been very well pointed out that America has always responded to our call most nobly. In fact, the relatives of those who live in Ireland assist them annually with large sums of money. From statistics that I have been enabled to collect since I have been in this country, I find that at least one-sixth part of the rent which has been paid to landlords of Ireland has been paid by Irish men and women living in America. You will see, then, that you also have an interest in trying to put an end to the system which cripples the resources of our country. The land system in Ireland puzzles many Americans.

They cannot understand how it is that there should be such an uproar every now and then about a few million acres of land over in Ireland when there is so much of it in this country for everybody to have at a very small price; and they invite our people over here. They say, "Give up your own lands, and find a home in our Western States. We shall be very glad to have you." Now, I think that this is a very great compliment to the Irish people. I think that the anxiety that has been shown by the newspaper press of the country during the last few weeks to persuade our people to emigrate instead of maintaining a firm grip on their homesteads, as we recommended them to do, is most complimentary to our people; and it is a very remarkable fact that the land system of Ireland should be such as to make the upper classes of that country desirous that the people should quit it, and that the land system in America should be such as to make Americans desirous that our people should come over here. I think such a statement by itself would be sufficient to condemn the Irish land system. The Irish land system, in common with that of England, is the feudal system of land tenure; and England and Ireland alone, of all the countries in Europe that originally started with this system, have persisted in maintaining it in its full vigor. Germany has abolished it in great part. France has entirely done away with it, and all the other nations of the continent have broken in and broken down this feudal system, more or less, because they have found that it throttles the industries of their country.

We have, in speaking in America up to the present time, confined ourselves chiefly to explaining the results of this system. We have pointed out that, although, as I have said before, Ireland is fertile and her climate good, yet the lands of Ireland are, for the most part, only half or one-third cultivated; that several millions of acres of that country are left entirely to waste, without any attempt at cultivation whatever; that the people engaged in agriculture are impoverished and discontented, and that every now and again famines sweep across the face of the country and carry away multitudes of starved wretches.

I propose to-night to go a little further, and to show to you some ways, some special methods — more than one method — which might be adopted in order to bring about the result we aim at; namely, the transfer of the soil of Ireland to the people who cultivate it. Now, I dare say, many of my hearers are aware that this programme of ours has been denounced in most unmitigated terms. We have been called Communists, and we have been told that we desire to plunder the landlords by wholesale; in fact, to rob them just in the same way that they have been robbing their tenants for the last four or five hundred years. In fact, our programme has been dealt with as if there were no precedents for such action, and as if the ownership of the soil by the people was a thing unheard of in the history of political economy; that when I tell you that already the legislatures of other countries have sanctioned the forcible expropriation of the soil from the landlords and its transfer to the tenants; when I point out to you some of the details by which this has been effected, and when I read to you some of the acts and edicts which have sanctioned its transfer, you will, I think, see that there is nothing which need press unduly upon any vested interests in Ireland.

I said just now that Germany had already partially abolished the feudal system of land tenure, the feudal system being one which gives the ownership of the soil to persons who generally live elsewhere, who do not occupy themselves in cultivating it, and gives to those who cultivate it only the right of paying as much rent as land-owners may choose to demand from them from time to time. Well, in Prussia this feudal system has been entirely abolished, and under these circumstances: In 1831, at the dawn of peace, when Prussia had just emerged from a disastrous and costly war, the king took counsel with his ministers as to how he might best secure the prosperity and the contentment of his subjects; and the result of it was that an edict was issued by the king of Prussia for the regulation of the relations between landlord and tenant.

When I read this edict I almost think I am reading the preamble of some of the bills that have been uselessly brought forward during the last few sessions of Parliament for the settlement of this important question. Now, this edict is a very remarkable one, and I should be glad if I may venture to trespass upon your time for a few seconds while I read the preamble to you. The preamble to the edict for the regulation of the relations between landlord and tenant recites as follows: " We, Frederick William, by the grace of God King of Prussia, having convinced ourselves by personal experience in our own domains, and by that of many lords of manors, of the great advantages which have accrued both to the lord and to the peasant by the transformation of peasant-holdings into proprietaries, and of the ameliorated condition of our subjects thereby on the basis of a fair indemnity, and having consulted in regard to this weighty matter experienced farmers and skilled persons of all kinds belonging to our province, and to the ranks of our subjects, ordain and decree as follows, among other things: that all tenants of holdings, whatever the size of the holdings, shall by the present edict become the proprietors of such holdings after paying to the landlord the indemnity affixed by this edict." Lower down comes a section in the following terms: "We desire that landlords and tenants should of themselves come to terms of agreement, and give them two years from the date of this edict to do so, and if within that time the work is not done the state will undertake it."

Well, then, I will now describe to you the way in which the state subsequently undertook to carry out the terms of this edict, upon the failure of the landlords and the tenants to come to any agreement upon the subject. By subsequent legislation a law was passed for the establishment of rent-banks. This law provided a method for the wholesale transfer of the lands held by the tenants, but belonging to the landlords, and by the instrumentality of these rent-banks, the state constituted itself a broker between the peasants, by whom the rents had to be paid, and the landlords, who had to receive them. Now, this was the course adopted: The banks established in each district advanced to the landlords debentures or bonds paying four per cent. interest on a capital sum equal to twenty years' purchase of what the state considered, through the valuation of its proper officers, to be a fair rent. The peasant paid into the hands of the district tax-collector monthly a sum equal to one-twelfth part of the annual interest at five per cent. on the amount of the purchase money, and he was compelled to continue these payments for forty-one years, and at the expiration of that time both principal and interest were discharged by these monthly payments. The landlord, on the other hand, as I have shown, received the debentures instead of the rent, amounting to twenty years' purchase of the fair value of the rent paid by the tenant, and, as you will see, he received nothing in cash. He simply received the obligation of the state in the shape of the debentures, and the state paid him four per cent. per annum in interest, and received from the tenants five per cent. per annum for forty-one years.

Now, the reason that no money was paid

by the Prussian state to the landlords was that it was a poor one; that it had no money to pay, and that it was not able to borrow any; but it did not allow its impecuniosity and bankrupt condition to stand in the way of the welfare of its people or reduce them to starvation. Nor did it allow any supposed superiority or rights of one class to stand in the way of the progress of the country at large and the contentment and prosperity of the subjects of the Crown. Now this is a system which has been practically carried into operation in the great country of Prussia, now the leading government of the continent; and, for my part, I see no reason why the same system should not be adopted as regards Ireland. We have to contend against the prejudices of the classes in that country who desire to maintain a social influence and prestige by the power of position which the absolute ownership of land, and of the tenants in that land, confers both in England and in Ireland; but I think that, as in other countries, when agitation has become sufficiently strong, when the situation has been made sufficiently difficult, that the government of England will step in; and that it will see, like the king of Prussia, that the time has come for it to make its Irish subjects contented and prosperous.

But there is another method which might be adopted in Ireland in order to bring about the same result, and which, perhaps, might be considered more desirous, although it necessitates the handing over of a large sum of money from the state to the landlords in the way of interest. This principle has been already partially sanctioned by the legislation of Great Britain under the Bright clauses of the land act of 1870. Mr. John Bright, the eminent reformer, asked, when Gladstone's land act was being passed, that a trial might be given and some opportunity afforded the Irish tenants to become the owners of their farms, and these Bright clauses were inserted in the act in order to afford that opportunity. Owing to the imperfections of these clauses, and the obstruction that the working of them has received from the Irish landlords who do not wish to see a peasant ownership or proprietorship established in Ireland, who do not wish to afford the working of such a scheme the slightest chance, they have remained a dead letter up to the present moment. I will shortly describe to you what these clauses are, in order that you may compare them with those ordained by the king of Prussia.

Under the Bright clauses of the land act, the state or government was empowered to advance to the tenants of proprietaries voluntarily sold by their landlords a sum equal to two-thirds of the purchase money paid by such tenants for their holdings, and the repayment by the tenant of the principal and interest of this advance was extended over a period of thirty-five years. Five per cent. per annum on the purchase price advanced by the government to the tenant was to be annually paid by the tenant to the government, and at the expiration of thirty-five years the tenant would have nothing more to pay; would have the land for himself, freed from all charge or encumbrance. Now, the tenants on the various estates that have come into the market since 1870 have been exceedingly anxious in every case to purchase; but in no single instance have they been permitted to do so. The landlord, when selling, has always preferred to sell his estate to a single person rather than take the trouble to divide it into small lots and sell it to his tenants, and he has in other ways obstructed the workings of these very beneficial clauses; but the clauses themselves are, to a very great extent, deficient in detail. They require to be considerably extended, and they only apply to estates which are voluntarily sold. Now, it is very evident that if we wait for the landlords of Ireland, all of them, to voluntarily sell their estates, and if the Irish tenants continue paying them, in an uncomplaining and patient way, rack-rents, why a very large number of landlords will never sell their estates at all; but no doubt we can compel, by indirect methods, landlords to sell their estates, and then they should be furnished to the Irish tenant.

But we require something more than that. We require to follow the example of the king of Prussia, and give the Irish landlords two years in which to transfer the land to the tenants, and if they do not attend to it in that time, then the government should step in and attend to the matter themselves. You will see, ladies and gentlemen, that I do not propose any radical method of settling the Irish land question. I have simply made an offer, a good offer, to the landlords; and I regret to see that they should be so foolish and so blind as to stand in their own light.

I feel convinced, that unless some method of this kind be adopted, and that very shortly, that the time is fast coming when the Irish landlords will have to go very much beyond that; but, being one of the number myself, I am naturally anxious to get as good a bargain as I can for them. In France the iron hand of revolution terminated the interests of landlords. Oh, I think there was also something about a lamp-post in that matter; and although I am not in favor of revolutionary methods, yet still, as a sensible man, I cannot help saying that if things are allowed to continue as they are in Ireland much longer, our people will scarcely be able to contain themselves, or to withstand the influences which must drive them towards violent and revolutionary measures. I hope that the government and the leaders may see their advantage while it is not too late. A million of money would be nothing for the English government to advance in settlement of this question, and they would receive every penny of it back with interest without the slightest degree of risk. To a government that does not hesitate to spend ten or twenty millions a year in childish and cruel wars in all parts of the world, it would be surely a good change if they would devote their attention to domestic affairs and to securing the happiness and prosperity of their own people at home, instead of destroying that of other people abroad. Now I have one word to say as to the advice that is offered to the American people by some of the newspapers. Now, I don't wish to be hard on the newspapers, or on that section of the press of New York which has given what I can only characterize as much degrading advice; but I have no fear that the people of this free land will listen to the recommendations that have been extended to them from that section.

You have been told that it is none of your business to interfere in the concerns of a foreign country, and I quite agree with that—that is none of the business of your government; but I also agree that it is not only the business but the duty of you to sympathize and assist us in our endeavor to redress a wrong which has been inflicted upon us by the government of England. One would think that the freedom of the press was suspended in this country as it is in England. You are not even to discuss this question. Why? Lest it might offend the British government. I can scarcely believe that I stand in a country which looks back to Bunker's Hill and Lexington. You were not afraid then to offend the British government, although you had just begun your career of freedom; and it struck me that this advice has not always been acted upon by England. I think I recollect at one time when you had an institution called slavery in operation in the United States of America, that you received a great deal of good advice from England upon the question. She was not afraid to tell you how sinful and wicked you were; and is it not also a fact that many of your distinguished men went over to England and lectured throughout the length and breadth of that land upon the institution over here? And I also think I can remember that when your civil war took place you received a great deal of advice, and something much more unpleasant than advice; I think that privateers were fitted out amid the applause of the governing classes of England to run the blockade.

In saying *au revoir*, ladies and gentlemen, I think it unnecessary for me to tell the present audience that it is their duty to sympathize with Ireland. I am confident that we have your sympathy. I believe that the public sympathy of this country is in our favor. Coming here as I do, and boasting American blood in my veins, I am proud of the success that has been recorded. I believe the heart of America is sound towards us, and that we shall receive both practical and sympathetic assistance in settling this question. I believe that you will give us money to keep our people from starving, and that you will give us the strength of that public opinion which will compel our rulers to do us justice. There are symptoms that this result has been already partially attained. Our government, up to the time that we had left Ireland, had persistently denied all along the existence or the imminence of famine in that country; now, scarcely a week after our arrival in America, it feels itself compelled to come forward and to announce that it is going to recommend Parliament to appropriate a quarter of a million pounds sterling to relieve the famine. Already the Duchess of Marlborough, the wife of the Lord Lieutenant of Ireland, an official who had stoutly denied to the last moment that there was any distress which the ordinary machinery of the poor laws could not relieve — she has appealed for assistance, in which she distinctly states that there is famine in Ireland, and that a great increase of it must be expected. Now, I say all this is directly due to public opinion that has been created in this country. The British government cannot afford to have its doings in Ireland exposed. It shrinks from the publicity which has attended, and must attend, our mission over here, and it is showing itself, although too late in my mind to get rid of the responsibility of the situation. I make a mistake when I say it is showing itself. It is pretending to show its interest. If it had been mindful of its responsibility it would have called Parliament together so as to relieve Ireland at once. They would have endeavored instantly to have reformed the wrongs of the landlords which have led to these horrible scenes and terrible sufferings; but they have done nothing of the kind. They say in two months time they will send over £250,000 to relieve the distress. What is to happen in the interval? We have information from certain sure sources to-day, all along the western shores of Kerry and northern Mayo, that thousands of persons will die of starvation in the next two months, unless they are immediately relieved. We are told that in some districts of Sligo and Galway the deaths will be in about the same rate they were in **1847-48**.

We must continue this agitation; we must continue to tell the truth about the relations between England and Ireland, until we force England still further — to do its duty and get some measure for the relief of the distress that has come upon us.

The speech was received with frequent manifestations of applause. Mr. Bennett of the "New York Herald" donated one hundred thousand dollars for relief of the famine, and a special committee was appointed to distribute this and the other donations received for the same purpose. The total aggregate of charity dispensed by their fellow-men all over the world, relieved the Irish people from the fell influence of famine, and excited in their breasts gratitude the most profound and enduring. Yet, interpreted from another point of view, every dollar contributed was a charge, by the nations of the earth, that England — be the reason what it may — had given incontrovertible proof that she was incapable of governing Ireland. The experiment had been tried for seven centuries; tried at times in a way that makes men sicken and pale at the memory, and that in the end went simply to show that if government is established for the greatest good of the smallest number, for pauperizing the many and enriching the few, for the partial administration of justice, then, and then only, had she any rightful claim to hold the reins of government in that country. Never had she made any concession under the influence of a feeling of right or justice; concessions have always been wrung from her when overawed by the organized physical force of the Irish people. So it was in 1782, when a quasi-independent Parliament was granted under the threats of the Volunteers. So it was in 1828, when the Duke of Wellington, through fear of civil war, had the Bill of Emancipation signed for his countrymen. So it was nearly fifty years ago, when the tithe tax was abolished. In 1845, before the hosts of Repealers were disbanded, Sir Robert Peel granted educational concessions; for there were diplomatic troubles, nay, menaces of war, between England and the United States, and between England and France, and it would be so easy, it was said, for either France or the United States to land an army in Ireland, where they would be assisted by nine-tenths of the inhabitants. Again, after the abortive Fenian insurrection, when the walls of Clerkenwell prison were blown down, and two prisoners released from a prison van, at mid-day, in the streets of Manchester, Mr. Gladstone, pointing to the events just mentioned, and apologizing for the necessity of the act, razed to the ground the Church by law established in Ireland.* The land act of 1870 was another tribute to the same sentiment. And what has been the fruit of the experiment? Not even Dead-Sea apples, shining and fair outside; but the sapless plant of extremest wretchedness, with famine gnawing at the heart-strings of millions of the people. Well might the nations of the earth charge that England was unfit to govern Ireland.

Meanwhile, there was a dissolution of the Beaconsfield ministry, and Mr. Parnell was obliged to go home in the interests of his constituents. They now represented all the

---

* 32 and 33 Vict., cap. 42.

tenant farmers in Ireland. Acting on his advice and that of his colleagues they had saved from fifteen to fifty per cent. of the exorbitant rents; the balance the landlords were mildly coerced to accept. With all this saving they had barely survived the terrible calamity, and still looked forward for redress to the law and the constitution. When the polling day arrived — voting by ballot is now the custom in Ireland — Mr. Parnell was elected representative by two counties, Meath and Mayo, and also one borough, the city of Cork. For prudential reasons he decided to sit for the borough. To show the tolerant spirit and absence of bigotry in the peasantry, it may be added that Rev. Isaac Nelson, minister of the Presbyterian church, from the province of Ulster, who professed the Land-League principles, was elected member for Mayo, one of the most Catholic counties in Ireland. It is related as a well-authenticated fact that, years and years ago in the same county, a Protestant minister, hearing of a visitation by his bishop, came to consult with the priest on the gravity of the situation. The minister and his sexton were the only members of the flock for some time, and if the bishop discovered this the incumbency would exist no longer. After thinking the matter over the priest said that his congregation would be dismissed in the forenoon, and he would lend them to the minister for the afternoon service. The people entered heartily into the plan, the bishop was charmed with so large a congregation, and the minister retained his incumbency.

Both in Great Britain and Ireland there was a sweeping Liberal victory at the elections, and Mr. Gladstone became Prime Minister. He was endeared to the Irish people even for the attempt to better their condition, and they nursed the fondest hopes that now, at last, a new dawn would overspread the country, and the darkness of night no longer overshadow them. They wanted the government to do what had been done by Russia, Prussia, Austria, Norway, Sweden, Denmark, and Belgium — buy off the vested rights of the landlords, and render them owners in fee, paying back principal and interest, running over a fixed number of years, until the amount invested was discharged in full. Some claimed that since the original taking was fraudulent, the title therefore was void, and no compensation should be given to the landlords, for they had no vested rights. And in this connection they alluded to the cargoes of tea thrown, incontinently, into Boston harbor. And later still to the emancipation of the slaves at the time of the American civil war, when vested rights were little thought of. But the general feeling was in favor of compensation. The subject was not free from entanglements; but the Irish and English statesmen in the House would, it was supposed, make a satisfactory adjustment of all equitable interests. Three hundred millions of pounds sterling, it was estimated, would be required to give compensation to all the landlords in Ireland. But some of them would never sell; they love the country, and wish to live and die there. And it would not be desirable to force these men to sell their estates.

But of the twelve thousand landlords mentioned by John Bright, some twenty-five per cent. are absentees, men who never, or very rarely, visit Ireland, and have no interest in the country other than to receive their annual rents. By the interaction of economic laws this has been a serious drain on the prosperity of the people. Again, there are large tracts of land owned by corporations, under patents coming down from the days of the plantation by James. And there are rack-renting landlords who have exterminated thousands and thousands of tenants, who have made and enforced the most arbitrary rules, and whose very presence, when it is not a public nuisance, creates a sense of the greatest irritation and bitterness in the minds of their neighbors. Get rid of such as these, by all means. We need not discuss the right of the government to take the lands for the public good; this was practically admitted by the tentative act of 1870, and proclaimed by Mr. Gladstone in a Midlothian speech during the late canvass. The law settles the matter by the principle of "eminent domain." But there are men in Ireland who clamor for the right of self-government. England has granted this to many of her colonies, and her foremost men profess that when the masses of a people demand it, it is tyranny to resist the wishes of the majority. When application of this principle is made to Ireland, however, there is always a very large beam in the English visual organ. In Bulgaria, Herzegovina, or Naples, such a principle works admirably; but the supremacy of English interest forbids mention of it as affecting Ireland.

There is a triple form of government for the colonies; in the Crown colonies, the English government has entire control of the legislation and of the appointment of public officers; in those that have representative institutions, the English government has simply the power of *veto* on legislation, but retains control of the appointment of public officers; while in those that have responsible government England exercises a power of veto on legislation, but has no control of any public officers other than its own representative. Under the last head are classified Canada, Newfoundland, Cape of Good Hope, New South Wales, New Zealand, Queensland, South Australia, Tasmania, Victoria, and Western Australia. They are held by such a weak thread, it is true, that it may snap asunder at any moment, unless England links them to herself by ties of mutual profit and advantage. Why, it is argued, cannot such a scheme as this be devised for the government of Ireland? The jealousy which England once felt of Irish trade and manufactures can no longer be entertained, for they are in the womb of the future, while she has now an assured and commanding place in the commerce of the world. If the matter were left to a popular vote to-morrow, the people would have such government by an overwhelming majority; and unless these professions of her foremost men are mere cant and hypocrisy, there is no good reason why Ireland should not have a responsible government.

But the leaders of the Land League have not sought even this. They struggled for reform in the system of land tenure, and by the means already alluded to. Over two hundred open-air meetings were held, and the peace and order of the country were seldom of better report. The agitation and organization still continued. Men in all parts of the country had come to regard the Land League programme as that by which alone any solid reform could be accomplished in their interests. Just at this time occurred an incident that has been widely spoken of. A certain Captain Boycott was agent for Lord Erne at Lough Mask, near Ballinrobe, in the county of Mayo. He was not a bad specimen of his class, imposing fines for leaving a gate open, for allowing a hen to fly over a fence, for leaving a wheelbarrow out of its place, for being one minute late at work in the morning, and for numberless other acts of equal importance. The amount collected for fines, deducted from the weekly pay of the laborer or tenant farmer who worked for him, told on the comfort of the family, and on the means of paying the rent. To so capricious an extreme had he gone, that the laborers, one and all, deserted him,— cook, chambermaid, ploughman,— all had gone; the butcher refused to sell him meat; the grocer, tea or coffee; the baker, bread. He was subjected to social and industrial ostracism, and the method adopted to do this was called " Boycotting."

Something analogous was done in England under Cobbett and his followers, when they forswore the use of all taxed articles, and a like spirit was manifested here before the Revolutionary War. In Ireland it spread like wildfire. To save his hay and turnips, and dig his potatoes, a number of Orangemen came from Ulster, under guard of a thousand English troops who had returned from fighting with Cetewayo. Large bodies of troops were concentrated in the neighborhood; for the government wished to precipitate a conflict, and let the blame rest on the impulsive character of the Irish. But the government was mistaken; the people showed good sense and self-control, and allowed the farce to go on without any other exhibition of feeling than a mood that made them laugh all over. The value of the crop was twenty-five hundred dollars, and it cost fifty thousand to harvest it.

Towards the close of the last century, " a

low class of Orangemen," known as "Peep-o'-day boys," were notorious for their midnight raids, ending in widespread destruction; but, of the better class, many belonged to the society of United Irishmen, and did good service to the cause. So it is to-day: the low class are ready to be made the tools of designing politicians, and to breed faction and disturbance; but the more intelligent and thrifty are going hand in hand with the land-leaguers to promote the good of their common country. The Liberal government arrested Mr. Parnell, Mr. Dillon, Mr. Biggar, Mr. Egan, and a number of others for conspiracy. Immediately the English press shrieked that the movement had come to an end. The most sensational stories were set afloat, — "Parnell would not dare to go to London at the opening of Parliament." "He would be arrested on sight, and sent back in chains to his trial." Perhaps the manner of furnishing the news will explain a good deal of this. There is a "central news agency" established in Dublin for the transmission of news to England; the contract between papers and reporters being, that the latter shall be paid for all of their telegrams used in the news columns of the papers. A spicy story of outrage, highly colored and seasoned, or some violent condemnation of government by a land-leaguer, is the most sought-for article, and the market is supplied by the enterprising knight of the quill. Thus are fabricated half the sensational rumors cabled over here as indisputable facts.

The trial took place; the chief justice, having prejudged the case, had the decency to retire from the bench. Judges Fitzgerald and Barry listened patiently to all the evidence of the government. When the defendants desired to introduce evidence in support of the truth of statements they had made on the hustings, and at public meetings, the chief count in the indictment was withdrawn by the government. It was plain that neither in the end they had in view, nor in the means taken to accomplish it, was there anything illegal; and the jury, by a vote of ten to two, were in favor of acquitting the accused of conspiracy. So the trial ended on the 25th of January of this year.

But there was another battle going on in the House of Commons. In the speech from the throne, the Empress of India devoted considerable attention to Ireland, and hoped facilities would be given the cultivators to get a proprietary interest in the soil. Several amendments were offered by the Irish members, but all in turn were voted down. For exercising their parliamentary rights they were called obstructionists, and the debate waxed warmer every day. A new rule was adopted to gag the Irish members; that is to say, if a member was named by the Speaker, he was suspended for that session; and if the naming was repeated, he would be suspended for a week. Mr. Parnell moved " that Mr. Gladstone be not heard," a motion made for the first time in two hundred years in the British House of Commons. It had been made the previous year by Mr. Gladstone against Mr. O'Donnell, in the debate on the character of the French minister, M. Lacour; but, probably on the suggestion of the Speaker, the motion and proceedings were then withdrawn. Mr. Parnell persisted, was named by the Speaker, and forcibly ejected by the sergeant-at-arms and his satellites. Mr. Dillon had been previously removed, in like manner, for pressing a motion on a point of order. The debate was on the coercion bill, and forcible removals continued, until the thirty-five members of the Land League party were outside the chamber. For seven weeks they fought day by day against the suspension of the Habeas Corpus Act, and now, in their enforced absence, it was rushed through the House. They had taken the precaution, in the interval, to transfer all the valuables and funds of the Land League to Paris, where Mr. Egan, the treasurer, now resides. Ireland is not unfamiliar with coercion acts. She has suffered deeply and long from every phase of British tyranny. Since 1830, forty-eight of these atrocious acts have been passed for her oppression. They were of varying degrees of severity, "*ex uno disce omnes.*" This is the text of the act now in force:—

" Be it enacted by the Queen's Most Excellent Majesty, by and with the advice and consent of the Lords spiritual and temporal and Commons in this present Parliament assembled, and by the authority of the same as follows:

"I.—1. Any person who is declared by warrant of the Lord Lieutenant *to be reasonably suspected* of having, *either before or after* the passing of this act, been guilty, as principal or accessory, of high treason, treason felony, or treasonable practices, *wherever committed*, or of any crime punishable by law committed in a prescribed district, being an act of violence or intimidation, or the inciting to an act of violence or intimidation, and tending to interfere with or disturb the maintenance of law and order, may be arrested in any part of Ireland and legally detained during the continuance of this act in such prison in Ireland as may from time to time be directed by the Lord Lieutenant without bail or mainprize, and *shall not be discharged or tried by any court* without the direction of the Lord Lieutenant, and every such warrant shall be conclusive evidence of all matters therein contained, and of the jurisdiction to issue and execute such warrant, and of the legality of the arrest and detention of the person mentioned in such warrant.

"2. Any person detained in pursuance of a warrant under this act shall be treated as a person accused of crime and not as a convicted prisoner.

"3. A list of all persons for the time being detained in prison under this act, with a statement opposite each person's name of the prison in which he is detained for the time being, and of the ground stated for his arrest in the warrant under which he is detained, shall be laid before each House of Parliament within the first seven days of every month during which Parliament is sitting.

"4. 'Prescribed district' means any part of Ireland, in that behalf specified by an order of the Lord Lieutenant for the time being in force; and the Lord Lieutenant, by and with the advice of the Privy Council in Ireland, may from time to time make, and when made revoke and alter, any such order.

"II.—1. Any warrant or order of the Lord Lieutenant under this act may be signified under his hand, or the hand of the Chief Secretary to the Lord Lieutenant, and a copy of every warrant under this act shall, within seven days after the execution thereof, be transmitted to the Clerk of the Crown for the county of the city of Dublin, and be filed by him in his public office in that city.

"2. The Lord Lieutenant, by and with the advice of the Privy Council in Ireland, may from time to time make, and when made revoke and alter an order prescribing the forms of warrants for the purposes of this act, and any form so prescribed shall when used be valid in law.

"3. Every order under this act shall be published in the 'Dublin Gazette,' and the production of a printed copy of the 'Dublin Gazette,' purported to be printed and published by the Queen's authority, containing the publication of any order under this act, shall be conclusive evidence of the contents of such order, and of the date thereof, and of the same having been duly made.

"4. The expression 'Lord Lieutenant'

means the Lord Lieutenant of Ireland, or other Chief Governor or Governors of Ireland, for the time being.

"III.—This act shall continue in force until the thirtieth day of September, 1882, and no longer."

During the debates a question was asked as to whether the government had opened letters of members on the Land League benches. The chief officer of the government evaded the question by speaking of the rights of the government. Now, this question, taken in connection with the answer, was a charge and an admission that the government had tampered with the mails. You may say that the law gives the chief representative of the government power to do so. Such a law makes provision for times of war or of treason; there has been no war, and not one treasonable act reported since 1871. Forty years ago, when Sir James Graham opened the letters of Mazzini, and avowed it, a sto m of indignation ran through Europe; but now, the character of "*Perfide Albion*" is known so well, such a tyrannical act does not cause even a ripple on the surface of public opinion. If that is the best form of government which is least felt by the governed,—and this is an axiom in political science,—has there been any people in history cursed with a worse form of government than the Irish? Under this act, man, woman, or child, if " reasonably suspected " of any of the offences mentioned, " wherever committed," is liable to arrest and detention in prison, without bail or trial, and to remain immured in such prison until the thirtieth day of September, 1882. Will not the man that has a private pique take advantage of the tyrannical law, and see to it that his neighbor is " reasonably suspected? " Will not the land agent of the absentee landlord fix the brand of suspicion on the independent tenant who will not doff his hat to him on the street, or refuses to pay him the exorbitant rent? Will not the eye of the government pry into every act, will not its ear listen to every sound, in order to bring the innocent victim within the meshes of its infamous machinery?

Truly a joyless and awesome life is that of the Irish people. They sow, but the landlords reap; they are simply the gleaners, the landlords gather in the harvest. If they agitate for the rights which God and Nature intended should be theirs, they are lodged in jail for disturbing the maintenance of law and order. But a supplementary bill called the "Irish Arms Act" renders their condition still more hopeless. In any proscribed district no man can have in his possession gun, pistol, revolver, or any such weapon. They were deprived of the right of free speech; they are now robbed of the right of self-defence. But it is claimed agrarian outrages justify resort to such extreme measures. Ireland has never, or seldom, been in a more peaceful state. Ejectments, evictions such as we spoke of a little while ago, form the gauge of agrarian outrages. The greater the number of evictions the larger will be the number of agrarian outrages. But in 1880, when Land League agitation was at its apogee, the number of outrages was proportionately small considering the number of evictions. During the first six months of that year, 1,696 heads of families were forcibly torn from their homes. Yet the whole number of outrages for the year was but 4,654. And what do these outrages consist of? Some, no doubt, were serious, and lamented and deprecated by the leaders of the Land League. There are few things more calculated to rouse the angry passions of any man than to be cast out, at the point of the bayonet, from the home of his childhood; to see his little holding, on which he has spent the labor and earnings of years, confiscated by the greed of a merciless landlord; to see his wife and family shivering on the roadside; his neighbors, by the rules of the estate, afraid to give them shelter from the storm. In the white heat of passion such a man, be he never so meek, will commit some outrages. But a large number of the reported outrages consist of threatening letters or notices. Many of these are vapid, meaningless things, and are, strictly speaking, outrages on paper. It is reported of a young lady who found the country somewhat monotonous, and desired to visit the capital, that a "threatening letter" to her father was the plan adopted for the change, and it was successful. Other such letters and notices are concocted by the *diablerie* of young men, thus furnishing a continual source of amusement. But compared with previous years, 1880, in the number of its agrarian outrages, no matter of what character, has been singularly free from outrages and crime. But 1881 bids fair to win for the English government a new patent for outrages. We have already glanced at the outrageous laws it has passed, and at the outrage it perpetrated on the parliamentary privileges of the Irish members. On the day preceding the commission of this last, it was guilty of another outrage: of arresting a man who had done more for the preservation of peace and order than its whole army in the island, of forty thousand men. Whatever of good, and true, and noble, and magnanimous a man can be well supposed to have, that had Michael Davitt. Whatever there is of purity and holiness in patriotism, that in a pre-eminent degree was a gift that he shared with his distinguished colleagues. This vile thing of a government, unable to see into the radiant soul of such a man, fastened its fangs upon him, and shut him up in a dungeon. Nor was it the first time that God's signet-mark of martyrdom for country was placed upon his brow. Over ten years ago, on May 14, 1870, he was arrested in London for Fenianism. He was tried in July and sentenced, by the late Chief Justice Cockburn, to fifteen years penal servitude. A gunsmith, named John Wilson, was arrested and tried together with him. John Wilson, a married man with a family, received a shorter sentence. Michael Davitt requested the judge to impose both sentences upon himself, saying that his fellow prisoner's connection with the case was a mere commercial one. The judge was touched with the unconscious magnanimity of the man, but could not grant the request. He was released on a ticket of leave in 1877, and revisited the States soon after the return of Mr. Parnell to Ireland. He lectured in various cities from New York to San Francisco, and here in Boston, on June 20th, delivered the following address: —

Mr. Chairman, Ladies and Gentlemen,— My first duty here to-night should be to offer an apology for obliging you to listen to the discussion of a subject which has been thoroughly threshed out. However, my being here is not a personal affair. I have simply come to excite your sympathy and obtain your assistance in a cause that has already appealed to your hearts and heads through the able and eloquent advocacy of one of the most popular Irishmen of the age, the head of the land movement itself, and the President of the Irish National Land League — Charles Stewart Parnell.

[After sketching the origin of the movement, the speaker said:]

The land reformers in Ireland are struggling in this movement under auspices more hopeful and conditions more encouraging than have ever before smiled on the cause of national effort. We have gathered under the banner of " The Land for the People " all that is most practical and earnest in the ranks of the Irish people. The movement knows no religious animosities in its government or its progress. It is non-sectarian without ignoring or infringing upon religion. It is national and patriotic while being social and non-political.

Its aims are conformable with the essence of justice itself, while the means employed to attain them can challenge the criticism of morality and reason. We have, of course, been called ugly names in the beginning, and have had motives attributed to us which were uncharitable and unmerited; but, conscious of the righteous work in which we were engaged, we encountered the misrepresentations of unjust critics with the convincing argument of practical work performed for a suffering people. The land movement is now in the proud and powerful position of having saved thousands of lives during this our fifth famine of the present century; of having for the first time in the sanguinary records of Irish landlordism brought the system to its knees, and compelled it to acknowledge the power of the democracy of Ireland, and of having brought over by firm but temperate opposition those of our prelates who first looked upon it as

"Confiscation," and saw nothing but "Communism" in the programme. With seventy or eighty of the best and most earnest priests in Ireland on the Land League; with the approbation of its platform and programme from the mouth of the illustrious archbishop, which is before the world, — we need not expect to hear any more ugly continental epithets heaped upon the land movement, or "Communistic Strollers" applied to land reformers.

[Mr. Davitt, after testing the various grounds upon which the people of Ireland rested their demand for the abolition of Irish landlordism, delivered a stirring invective against emigration as a remedy for the social evils of Ireland, and supported his position by asserting that injustice and tyranny must be confronted whenever and wherever they strike at the rights of industrial humanity.]

Why, instead of being asked to leave Ireland by our friendly American critics, should we not be encouraged to drive out the system which robs and humiliates us there? If an unjust and immoral power, such as Irish landlordism, is to be allowed the right of plundering an industrious people, and driving them like dumb animals from the land of Ireland, what encouragement would this not be to land monopoly here in America and elsewhere. But we are not going to abandon the old country so readily as all that. Poor and afflicted as she now stands before the civilized world, she is a prize worth struggling for — a land worth clinging to for herself alone; and though thousands may be forced by want and necessity to follow the track of the setting sun, millions will remain to assert their right to live in the land upon which God placed them, and destroy the system which now tramples upon that right. In one hundred years, there have died in Ireland through starvation alone, under this system, no less than 2,500,000 of our people. One hundred and twenty years ago the annual rental of Ireland was £2,000,000, or $10,000,000. The annual rental of Ireland to-day is from £15,000,-

000 to £20,000,000, or $75,000,000; so that, in the space of one century, the tax imposed upon her industry by Irish landlordism is 750 per cent. In that period no less a sum than £3,500,000 has been stolen from Ireland by the lazy, idle, and morally worthless landlords.

Admitted, then, that this system is wrong, the question is, How are we to abolish it? It will not be abolished by mere wishing. Something more is required. Landlordism is one of the greatest powers for evil that has ever cursed God's earth. The landlords of Ireland are not numerically a strong class; but they have behind them the prestige of the British empire. [A voice: "Money, organization, and bayonets."] My friend says, by money, organization, and bayonets. Well, we have commenced the organization already. If organization will not settle the question, and the other parts of the advice have to be resorted to, the Irish landlord and the English government must accept the responsibility. In the past, the Irish tenant farmers have been divided, or rather, no political party came to the front to stand between them and their enemies. They were told that by and by their rights would be regained; but until the tenant farmer could be shown a power superior to the landlord, he never placed any faith in the promise that the land would be free. He wanted to see some power which would stand between him and the evicting power of the enemy of his homestead and children. This has now been supplied him by combination among his own class, and hence the determined spirit which has been exhibited by the tenant farmers of Ireland during the past twelve months.

The Land League proposes that a branch of its body shall be started in every parish in Ireland, and that the tenant farmers in all those parishes must enrol themselves in that mission to strike down the system. This will be a protecting power to the tenantry in the locality. If the landlord attempts to crush a single tenant, the theory of the bundle of sticks will be put into practice.

The next plan in connection with this movement is the corner plank of the Land

League platform. After 1848, when the peasant class were almost crushed by the exactions of the landlords and the ravages of the famine, they could be easily thrown out because other farmers would take the holdings; but to-day, from east to west, from north to south, not a man could be found who would dare to take the farm of an evicted tenant. If one should be found so recklessly indifferent to his own fate, it would be simply impossible for him to live unmolested in that locality. The people would not buy from him; they would not sell to him; in chapel on Sunday he would have to sit apart by himself; and this spirit has got such a firm hold of the people that I venture to say that to-day there is not a man in Ireland who would follow the example of those of 1848. The vacant farms will remain vacant, and be a standing warning to the landlords that eviction will not pay.

But it may be asked, What is to become of those who will be turned out on the roadside? Those, thanks to the liberality of our banished brethren on this side of the water, will be cared for. Thanks to your helping hands, the Land League can now protect the evicted families in Ireland. No sooner is a struggling farmer and his wife and children turned out by the landlord, than the fact is known to the Land League in Dublin, and they are protected.

What can the landlords do under those circumstances? They will not have the satisfaction of seeing their victims starve. Nay, they will not have the satisfaction of driving our people out of the country, or into the demoralizing sub-institution of landlordism, the workhouse, if the Land League can help it. The cable informed us the other day, that in the little village of Balla, in the county of Mayo, a family was evicted by the constabulary, but the same evening one thousand men came and reinstated them. The money sent by the people of Boston will help to keep the lands of the evicted farmers unoccupied. From platform, pulpit, and press is being preached the crusade. From north to south, from east to west, every Sunday you will find little land meetings being held. In every churchyard after church is over, in every roadside, and every crossway in Ireland, if you meet tenant farmers, they are discussing the land question. Not with bated breath, as in by-gone days. There is no fear, no doffing the hat to every titled scoundrel, as in by-gone days. The manhood of Ireland has been evoked to crush out the slavishness that disgraced the Irish people in past years. In addition to all this, we are creating an audience for this question throughout the civilized world.

This reform is not a novelty in the world. It is something that has been accomplished in other countries, to take the land from a dissolute and idle class and hand it over to a moral and industrious class. Peasant proprietary has supplanted landlordism in every other civilized country. We have demanded it for Ireland also, and are resolved to work for it in a way that will not admit of failure. We know by bitter past experience how unscrupulous our enemy England is, and we are resolved to sap and undermine her Irish garrison of landlordism while keeping out of the range of our enemies' guns. This outwork of alien misgovernment brought to the earth, our people can then plant the standard of national effort upon solid and secure foundations. While working out this land problem in Ireland we are performing pioneer duty for other land-crushed peoples, and aiding the cause of humanity throughout the world

After appealing to the audience to push on the Land League movement in Boston, Mr. Davitt resumed his seat amidst loud applause.

He has stated that he was convicted on perjured testimony, and to those who know the man this statement will be conclusive of the fact. But it receives unexpected confirmation from the lately published reminiscences of an ex-superintendent of the Dublin police. In this book it is related that the Crown witnesses for State trials are in the habit of preparing themselves for their work by means of a " mock trial " or mootcourt. Here they are cross-examined, and taught by the detectives how best to perform, each his part, in the life-drama to be acted next day before a jury. When shall roll the lava-tide of retribution to scorch and burn and destroy a power so monstrous as to be guilty of this diabolical iniquity?

For one year and eleven months this movement has been gathering strength, numbering in its ranks hundreds of thousands, and not the flash of a sword, or click of a rifle has once disturbed the harmony of the proceedings. Of the outrages complained of, many were manufactured of the whole cloth; others consisted of boys whistling contempt at landlords. But the government is arraigned for an outrage the most flagitious,— arresting a man whose voice, always potential, was never raised save to promote peace, friendship, and unity. Nor can it be alleged that he had violated the conditions of his ticket of leave; the charge was made by Lord Randolph Churchill a short time before the arrest, and publicly repudiated by Mr. Foster. The people, in thousands, assembled in England and Ireland to denounce so flagrant a breach of honor, and Mr. Dillon,

M. P. for Tipperary, at the first public meeting of the Irish National Land League thereafter, delivered the following address:—

Gentlemen,—On hearing last night of the arrest of Michael Davitt, it occurred to me immediately that it would be a most desirable thing that a special meeting of the Irish National Land League should be immediately summoned in order to convey to the people of Ireland what they thought of the arrest of Michael Davitt; and also, with the fullest authority of the body, of conveying their opinion as to what ought to be the attitude of the people, and what, in fact, it was essential should be the attitude to hold with regard to this arrest in order not to interfere with the success of the cause he, as well as we, have so much at heart. Now, with regard to what we think of the arrest of Mr. Davitt, my opinion is exceedingly strong — upon that I have not the slightest doubt — that this arrest is to be accounted for in the following way: I believe that the government in Ireland — that is to say, the staff of Dublin Castle — got alarmed at the length of time which we had succeeded in delaying the passage of the coercion bills. I believe they got further alarmed by the fact, which was becoming more and more evident every day, that outside the Liberalism of England there was among the working people a large and extending opinion hostile to these coercion acts. They began to see that if we could succeed in holding coercion bills at bay for a longer period — for a couple of months — while we carried on the meetings in the centres of industry, and whilst also the accounts of outrages in Ireland ceased in this country; whilst it was in a state of absolute peace — a condition in which Michael Davitt was largely instrumental in keeping it; they began to see that the people of England would begin to ask themselves, "What are we passing coercion bills for?" and the result would be that coercion would fall through. I have not the least doubt in my mind that the object of the arrest of Michael Davitt was the hope they have raised both by withdrawing his powerful influence over the people and by the natural irritation and anger it would excite amongst our people that it would lead to the commission of such acts of violence as would facilitate the hurrying through of coercion acts. Our object is to make, through the press, an appeal of the most earnest character to the people of Ireland and England not to allow themselves to be made the victim of this conspiracy; that they will maintain the attitude they have maintained up to the present, and resist this attempt to drive them off the field of battle which they have hitherto occupied into a field of battle to which their enemies would drive them, and in which they would crush them. They would ask that every one who sympathizes with the Land League will keep from acts of violence, no matter what the provocation; that he will exert himself to put a stop to all violence of every kind, and exert himself strenuously to do so, in order that we may be successful in our attempt to hold the ground which Michael Davitt and the League selected, and on which we so far have succeeded in fighting the battle of the League.

One of my chief objects to-night was to

come and make an appeal to the Irish people that they will show as much self-control, as much patience, as much endurance of insult, and even of suffering, as they have hitherto of courage, and sometimes of too reckless courage, in the cause of their country. There is just as much courage — a great deal higher kind of courage — in knowing when to control yourselves, when to endure patiently, as there is in striking a blow, or in taking your life in your hand and going out into the field against the foes of your country. [After referring to the coercion bill, and justifying the action of the Irish members, Mr. Dillon proceeded to say a word about what occurred last night.] The English papers are ashamed of what occurred last night, and have endeavored grossly to misrepresent the whole transaction. They stated that we came down to the House prepared with a deliberate conspiracy to go through the scene enacted last night. That is perfectly false. None of us had the smallest intention of doing anything but fairly debating Mr. Gladstone's resolution. In fact, we had resolved not to speak at all that night, but to leave the debate to the Whigs and Tories between them. But just as question time was over we received a telegram announcing Mr. Davitt's arrest. Mr. Parnell arose in his place and asked the question which you have all read. He asked the question, What condition of his ticket of leave has Mr. Davitt violated? And the government being ashamed of the whole transaction, Sir Vernon Harcourt adopted the unprecedented course of instantly sitting silent and refusing an answer. Now, this was unprecedented in the House. It was an act of gross discourtesy. I have never seen it done to any man, not to say a man in the position of Mr. Parnell, who is the leader of a considerable party. Sir Vernon Harcourt sat silent and deigned no answer to the question. Mr. Parnell waited for a few minutes to receive his answer, and then rose again with the intention of moving the adjournment of the House in order to call attention to this gross act of discourtesy on the part of a Minister. The Speaker deliberately passed him over, grossly violating the well-known laws and regulations of the House, and called on Mr. Gladstone to address the House. The Speaker, deliberately calculating on the temper of the House, and denying Mr. Parnell the privilege which the humblest member of the House has — not at the Speaker's call, but of right, as the representative of the people — passed him, refused to hear him, and called on Mr. Gladstone to address the House. When Mr. Gladstone rose, Mr. Parnell gave way to the chair. I rose to a point of order, the point of order being that Mr. Parnell was in possession of the House, and not Mr. Gladstone. Now, it is a well-known custom of the House of Commons that no matter who is speaking — and the highest officer or Minister has in this respect no more rights than the humblest private member — if you rise to a point of order you have a right to insist on being heard. The Speaker can rule against your point of order, but he has no right to refuse to hear you. What did he do in my case? He refused to hear me. I sat down and gave way to the chair. Then Mr. Gladstone sat down. He passed me over and called on Mr. Gladstone again. I gave way again. I rose again and sat down a third time. The fourth time, when he deliberately refused me my right to speak on a point of order in order to stifle discussion on the arrest of Mr. Davitt, of which the government were thoroughly ashamed, I stood against the chair and claimed privilege. Now, what occurred afterwards, I had nothing to say to, but I don't regret it. We must take into account what is perhaps not known in Ireland, namely, that when the Irish Secretary said "Yes, sir," in answer to Mr. Parnell's question, he did so with a tone of insolent triumph which wounded every Irishman in the House who had any feeling for his country. His words were backed with a cheer, which was an act of the most contemptible cowardice — a cheer from the Liberal benches — as if they had defeated a great army in the field, instead of having only seized on one man who offered no resistance. They cheered in the most enthusiastic way an act they ought to have been thoroughly ashamed of.

So that I think the action of the Irish members will never make them less popular, at all events in Ireland.

Now I have got a word to say in conclusion, and it is this: After we left the House — after we were removed from the House — Mr. Gladstone rose in his place, and I regret to say that he was enabled, by the treachery of a few, to announce that we were a fraction of the Irish representation — a contemptible minority. Who put it into his mouth to say that of the Irish representation? The Irish people at the last election returned to the House sixty-five men — that is to say, a majority of nearly twenty — pledged every man of them, up to their very lips, to act with the Irish party. They got their seats on that pledge, and, like traitors, they broke their pledge because we would not adopt their views. We did nothing to justify them in that. We held a fair meeting in Dublin, and they would not submit to the party. They broke their pledges to their constituents, and they deserted us in the most difficult hour of the struggle; and I say now unhesitatingly that were it not for that desertion the Irish Coercion Bill would never have passed the House. If we could stand as we were, a clear majority of the representatives of the Irish people, no Minister, however powerful, could press the bill through the House. But these men selected this opportunity to desert their party, which they had solemnly pledged themselves to support, and put it in the mouth of the Ministers to call us a fraction, and to point out, when we were removed from the House, that the obstruction to the coercion bill came only from some fraction of the representatives of the Irish people.

Well, now, all I can say is, that I shall be very much disappointed with regard to these men, if the Irish people do not take immediate steps to show to the public opinion of England that this cave of traitors—because they deserve no other name but traitors—do not represent their constituents, but that we represent their constituents as well as our own constituents, as we have taken the liberty of asserting in the House. And though this League has wisely abstained from interfering in parliamentary matters, it would act equally wisely now in taking this step, inasmuch as we have been deserted in an attempt to protect this organization from a bill directly aimed to destroy it; and I think that this League ought to put its machinery in force in order to give voice to the public opinion of the constituents of those men in condemning this shameful act of treachery —I will say one of the most disgraceful acts of treachery in Irish history—after the great exertions the people have made. I have just two words to say in conclusion with regard to the people: We have to face the fact that a new departure has been made by the government. The arrests have begun, and of course none of us can tell where they will stop. The probability is that the government, having turned their back on shame and the pretension of being a Liberal government, will arrest numbers of the League—perhaps the whole executive of the League. We don't know how many they may arrest, and therefore it is wise that we should say a word or two of counsel to the people. Some discussion has arisen on the question of what the people ought to do in reference to rent in case the executive of the League was arrested. Now, the advice I would give to the people is this: In any locality where the local executive of the League is arrested, and the organization is broken up, let the members of that branch pay no more rent until the executive is liberated, and justice done to them. I do not think it would be wise to advise the people to anything like a general strike against rent, because I wish to give every landlord the opportunity of taking his stand either for or against coercion. If the landlords of a locality are men enough—if they have a kindly feeling for the people, and keep the hand of coercion from that locality—let them have what they have had up to this—justice. But if they declare war on the people of that locality, and bring in the coercion act, and arrest the executive, let the people declare war on them in the only way in which they can do so. That is the first piece of advice I give. The second is this: Whenever a landlord makes himself prominent in demanding coercion, or in approving of the arrest of Mr. Davitt, or in any way of the present policy of the government—if he makes himself prominent, and if your organization includes his estate—let us cut off his supplies. By that means we shall be in a position to reward those who refuse to declare war on the people, and to punish those who do declare war against them. If a landlord acts kindly, and does not by word or deed encourage the policy of coercion, let us not strike against him, but treat him with justice. I say, in conclusion, that the people need not in the least be alarmed at the threat of coercion. The one thing necessary all over the country is this: that if they should be arrested they must go to prison peaceably, and endure a little for the sake of their country. If their wives and their families suffer through their imprisonment, as long as we have a pound in our treasury, and I am happy to say we have a great many pounds now, we shall see that their wives and their families don't suffer from their absence. We must remember that the policy of the League can be carried out if all the executives were arrested; and that the only thing that the people have to fear is being excited. Patient endurance is the policy which has won so far—patient endurance and submission to imprisonment, and patient determination to go on with the movement, is the advice which Michael Davitt would give them. The best way to avenge, if we can avenge, as I believe we shall avenge, the arrest of Michael Davitt, is to pursue the policy which he counselled to the people, till we have brought the landlords to their knees, and till we have overthrown that system which he has offered up his life to overthrow.

But the indignation and resentment were not confined to England and Ireland; they burst forth in thunder-tones from a thousand platforms and official bodies in the United States. An enlightened public opinion, with a sound like a trumpet of war, told haughty England that nor Star Chambers nor *léttres de cachet* would be tolerated at this stage of the nineteenth century; that uncivilized means of ruling a civilized people was an international wrong; that the use of such means was biting at a file, and if such means were persisted in that file would be used to sharpen instruments of agony that would torture her to death. England cowered at the threat, and it was announced that prison discipline was changed in Mr. Davitt's favor; that "he was satisfied with his treatment."

Satisfied? Let us inquire how England treated the untried political prisoners in 1867. The official report of Mountjoy Prison says for that year: "I object on medical grounds to the punishment of prisoners by giving them insufficient clothing, as one not only likely to develop scrofulous disease; but highly likely to give rise to acute disease also. One prisoner had the appearance of a man laboring under serious illness; indeed, the leaden hue of his face, and sunken eye, looked like that of a patient struck with Asiatic cholera. I inquired what ailed him: he said that he was cold—very cold; that no bed nor bedding, except a single rug, had been allowed him during the night; that he had lain on the floor with no other bed-clothes than a rug to cover him; and that he was cold into his very bones. About the time referred to the weather was exceedingly inclement. The cold was on some nights intense — several degrees below the freezing point. The weight of the rug allowed to the prisoner I ascertained to be not more than four pounds. He had nothing but the floor to lie on — no bed-clothes, mattress or pillow." Dr. McDonnell, the superintendent for several years, and president of the Irish College of Surgeons, was discharged for letting some light fall on the inner management of the prison. Mr. Davitt himself has written and spoken of the manner in which he was treated before, and there is nothing more brutal or revolting conceivable. Now, under the coercion act, numbers of men are inhumanly maltreated, wrenched from their homes and families, and buried in those prisons. The women of Ireland have organized to procure funds for the families of the prisoners, and for the support of those who are evicted. Their first public meeting was held at Claremorris on the 20th of last month, and Miss Anna Parnell, sister of the president of the

League, spoke, at an open-air meeting, on the duties of the hour, and of the good that could be accomplished by the women. A branch of the League was formed. She has since spoken at Mullingar, and other places, with telling effect.

One of the results springing from Mr. Parnell's visit to the States was the establishment of an auxiliary League. Before leaving New York for Ireland, he had conferred with men in various parts of the Union, and recommended the organization of such a League. On May 18th and 19th of last year they met together at Trenor Hall, N. Y., drew up appropriate resolutions, elected officers, and adopted a provisional constitution. For a variety of reasons Rev. Lawrence Walsh, of Waterbury, Conn., treasurer, had to conduct the entire executive business. A call was issued for the convention of delegates of the various branches to meet at Buffalo, where the convention was held on the 12th and 13th of January last. Though in numbers not very large, yet never assembled together in the States a more intelligent or representative gathering to take counsel together on the welfare of Ireland. One of the city papers observed of the delegates that "they would do honor to any country or any cause." Having transacted the business for which they met, cemented the bonds of friendship and unity, and adopted fitting resolutions, they elected as Central Council Hon. P. A. Collins, president of the organization; re-elected as treasurer, Rev. Lawrence Walsh; and elected as secretary, Thomas Flatley, Esq. The election gave general satisfaction. It would be premature to speak of the work they have done. They have put the harness on; let it be told, when they put it off, what energy, resolution, and ability can do to bring about the consummation we have all so much at heart. It is, however, to the spontaneous zeal and unchangeable love of Ireland that animate the tens of thousands of members, that we must look for ultimate triumph.

Men of Irish birth or lineage, clerical and lay, were never so thoroughly consolidated, at home or abroad, as in this movement for the social and political regeneration of Ireland. It has enlisted, too, the activities and sympathies of the women in the United States. The soul of this organization is the revered mother of the leader of that Spartan band that is battling with such heroism for the rights of their country. Mrs. Delia T. S. Parnell has eschewed no toil, no difficulty, in this work; her wonderful skill and rare tact have been supremely successful. She has organized over forty branches, and is still unceasingly employed. Her labors have been sweetened by the object in view, and she has had a valuable ally in Miss Ford, of New York. Perhaps the chief good to result from this movement is the love it will implant in the rising generation for the land of their forefathers, the knowledge it will impart of the question at issue, the fact that it will tend to enlighten public opinion, and imbue the minds of mothers of a coming Irish-American generation with ideas and principles that will be bone of the bone and flesh of the flesh of their children. Must that generation take up the work left undone by those gone before them, or have we now the men of intrepid daring, consummate prudence, and unbending resolution to put an end forever to the seven-century struggle?

The Irish are not engaged in a fight for total separation from England. They have acted within constitutional lines to recover their natural rights,—life, liberty, and the pursuit of happiness. England that claims to be the champion of liberty tramples out the last shred of it enjoyed by the Irish, manacles their limbs, makes of their country a military barrack, and denies to the tenants any measure of legal relief that would be a guarantee of comfort or happiness. Why may not a congress of the nations, under sanction of international law, take steps to abolish this odious deprivation of natural rights, the Nessus shirt in which tyrants enswathe a subject nation? Or is there living to-day a De Beaumarchais in Europe, or America, that, fired with enthusiasm himself, will make his country glow with the same feelings, and inspire it with confidence in the dawning independence of Erin? It would be policy for England to grant the concessions now demanded. It may be argued that her future is intertwined with that of Ireland, and therefore it would be suicidal on her part to permit total separation. Why not then preserve the nexus of the empire, and give to Ireland the right of self-government? Under intense provocation the Irish have shown admirable self-control; they have the best governed municipalities in the three kingdoms; under presentments of grand juries their roads, bridges, and other kindred works are well managed, and there is a tolerably good system of administration of the poor law by unpaid Boards of Guardians elected by the people. Every motive of policy, and every principle of justice, alike, demand the amplest rights of self-government. England exults in her massive strength, her almost irresistible power; and yet by permitting feudal despots to lord it over millions of the Irish people she visits them with periodical famine, and brings on chronic discontent reaching to the perilous edge of civil war. Ireland wisely abandons the arbitrament of arms to secure her constitutional rights. She demands a redress of grievances, and for agitating this question her children are cast into prison, and denied the right of trial by jury. Martyrs were imprisoned and put to death before the Labarum, "*en touto* NIKA," shone refulgent in the sky. Men ready to surrender their liberty and their lives in any good cause, God, in time, will reward with a crowning victory. So shall it be with the men of Ireland. She has the moral sympathy of all nations — perhaps would have material aid, also, in an emergency; but her own indomitable courage and self-reliance must be the chief factors in her disenthralment.

> "A nation freed by foreign aid
> Is but a corpse by wanton science
> Convulsed like life, then flung to fade —
> The life itself is self-reliance."

She has taken this lesson to heart, and the character of her sons is moulded by the teaching. Impulse is tempered by prudence, rashness gives way to careful forethought, for disregard of consequences is substituted the doctrine of probabilities, and over all beams the light of a daily increasing intelligence.

Ireland uses moral force to effect a peaceful revolution. The press is a microscope by which the world can see the galling wrongs which she has endured. But if a real battle of Dorking should be fought, and a foreign army landing on the shore should lay waste the towns of England and scatter her forces, the wail of Ireland's anguish would be the requiem of her greatness, the flame of Irish discontent would cover her surface as with the scoriæ of a volcano. Unless might be right it is fighting against the inevitable to withhold the reasonable demands that are now made. Coercion laws are a proof of incapacity to govern; let the Irish people govern themselves, frame laws for the common weal, adjust conflicting claims and interests, provide for the manifold exigencies that may arise, and give to all, Catholic and Protestant, Trojan or Tyrian, the man in the cabin or in the castle, equal and exact justice, a full and comprehensive charter for political, civil, and religious liberty. Then, as with an organ peal of world-wide volume, would alleluias of joy resound over the earth, for the dwelling-place of the Irish race has, now, no boundaries other than those of the earth itself.

It is too late to account for the criminal negligence and maladministration of the government by alleged idiosyncrasies of the governed; the day for such fallacious reasoning has gone, never to return. Even in British Colonies that enjoy responsible governments, the Irish emigrants and their descendants have displayed the highest qualities of manhood and of citizenship, and in the United States they have shown a native thrift, industry, and intelligence that have redounded to the welfare and prosperity of the republic. None show a deeper love, a more profound appreciation of free institutions. Therefore are they leagued together with invincible will and purpose, to break the fetters of thraldom by which their brethren are enslaved, to aid in procuring for them a large measure of those blessings which they themselves enjoy. Let the relation of Ireland to the British empire be somewhat like unto that which each State bears to the general government at Washington. There may be defects in the machinery of our system; it is still ripening more and more to maturity. Perhaps in English and Irish statesmanship there is sufficient astuteness and skill to observe what is wanting in the model, and to render the copy the perfect flower of federal relations. For the rest, let not the glamour of power blind the minds of rulers to the inexorable demands of right and justice. On these, as upon a rock, the people base their demands for the abolition of a land code, the most iniquitious and indefensible sanctioned by any civilized nation. There is a quaint Irish proverb which says, "The cows die while the grass is growing"; this grass of reform has been looked for with straining eyes; there has been nothing to gladden the prospect, nothing to shield the people from the storm of tyranny save that rock of right and justice on which its fury beat in vain,—a rock that has withstood all the tempests of ages, and is the sheet-anchor with which will sail into port that sacred bark, freighted with the regeneration and freedom of Ireland.

It can hardly be said Mr. Gladstone has his party so well in hand that a satisfactory land bill will be passed. The inveterate selfishness of the House of Lords is an insuperable barrier to the passage of such a measure. They are all extensive landowners, many with titles derived from confiscations, and with them personal interests are paramount to the good of the empire. For such reasons they rejected last year the " Compensation for Disturbance " bill. There should be a radical change in this fossil institution. It contains, it is true, men whose social prominence is equalled only by their intellectual ability or knightly attributes; but with these we find associated a parcel of mummies that can never be galvanized into sympathy with any measure of progress or enlightenment; least of all can they be quickened into advocacy of a bill that would take one dime from a rent-roll, or do equity to a class whom, under the " *odisse quem læseris* " maxim, they hate with an hereditary hatred. Ministries may split upon this Irish question, and each successive failure to solve it will lead to another dissolution. But for the honor of the Irish race, for the vindication of its manhood and intelligence, the Land League agitation must go on, no backward step be taken; all the members, linked together by memories of the past and hopes of the future, must show a solid and united front, no faltering or flinching by internal dissensions, or abuse from without; and so soldered together we shall at last see a redeemed and transfigured Ireland. Her indestructible spirit shall body forth its old-time grandeur; anointed by the sacrament of self-government she shall return to the ways of her youth, and become to the countries of the globe the foster-mother of science, sanctity, freedom, and civilization.

APPENDIX.

APPENDIX.

CRIMINAL STATISTICS.

Number of Offenders committed for trial, convicted, and acquitted in England, Scotland, and Ireland in each of the five years ending 1879.

YEAR.	England and Wales.		
	Committed for trial.	Convicted.	Acquitted.
1875,	14,174	10,954	3,714
1876,	16,078	12,195	3,841
1877,	15,890	11,942	3,903
1878,	16,373	12,473	3,864
1879,	16,388	12,525	3,835

Scotland.

1875,	2,872	2,205	647
1876,	2,716	2,051	607
1877,	2,684	2,009	642
1878,	2,922	2,273	652
1879,	2,700	2,091	606

Ireland.

1875,	4,248	2,484	1,748
1876,	4,146	2,343	1,789
1877,	3,870	2,300	1,559
1878,	4,182	2,292	1,879
1879,	4,363	2,207	2,146

Number of Inhabited Houses in Ireland.

Total in 1841,	1,328,839
Total in 1871,	961,380

Decrease in the various Provinces.

In Leinster,	from 306,459 to 227,462
In Munster,	from 364,637 to 234,757
In Ulster,	from 414,551 to 345,464
In Connaught,	from 243,192 to 153,697

Number of Emigrants from Ireland from the 1st May, 1851 to 31st December, 1879.

From Leinster,	478,002
From Munster,	886,686
From Ulster,	750,426
From Connaught,	315,941
Counties not stated,	110,615
Total,	2,541,670

Board of National Education.

Number of Schools and Pupils in attendance from 1870 to 1879.

Years.	No. of Schools.	No. of pupils in attendance.
1870,	6,806	950,999
1871,	6,914	972,906
1872,	7,050	960,434
1873,	7,160	974,696

Number of Schools — Continued.

Years.	No. of Schools.	No. of pupils in attendance.
1874,	7,257	1,006,511
1875,	7,267	1,011,799
1876,	7,334	1,032,215
1877,	7,370	1,023,617
1878,	7,443	1,036,742
1879,	7,522	1,031,995

Parliamentary Representation.

The country is represented in the Imperial Parliament by 28 temporal peers, and 103 commoners; of which latter class 64 represent the 32 counties, 2 Dublin University, 12 the cities and towns of Dublin, Cork, Limerick, Waterford, Belfast, and Galway; and 25 the boroughs.

Judicial Divisions.

The judicial establishment of Ireland is now fixed by the Supreme Court of Judicature, which constitutes and amalgamates all the other high courts.

The Superior Courts are held in Dublin.

Two of the judges hold assizes for criminal and civil pleas in each county in spring and summer every year, for which purpose the country is divided into six circuits.

Population from 1841 to 1871.

In 1841 the population amounted to 8,196,597, and in 1871 the number was 5,412,377.

Decrease in the Various Provinces.

Leinster, from 1,982,169 to 1,339,451.
Munster, from 2,404,460 to 1,393,485.
Ulster, from 2,389,263 to 1,833,228.
Connaught, from 1,420,705 to 846,213.
Total decrease, 2,784,220.

Between 1841 and 1851 the population decreased about one-fifth, — 19.79 persons in every hundred; from 1851 to 1861, 11.79 per cent; and from 1861 to 1871, 6.67 per cent.

EXTENT OF LAND IN STATUTE ACRES UNDER THE FOLLOWING CEREAL CROPS IN IRELAND IN EACH YEAR FROM 1870 TO 1879.

YEAR.	WHEAT.	OATS.	POTATOES.	FLAX.
1870, . .	259,847	1,650,039	1,043,583	194,910
1871, . .	244,451	1,636,136	1,058,434	156,670
1872, . .	225,294	1,624,711	991,871	121,992
1873, . .	167,554	1,510,972	993,262	129,297
1874, . .	187,978	1,480,897	892,425	106,907
1875, . .	158,995	1,501,867	900,586	101,174
1876, . .	119,700	1,487,166	880,716	132,938
1877, . .	139,297	1,476,172	873,291	123,380
1878, . .	154,041	1,412,845	846,712	111,817
1879, . .	157,511	1,330,261	842,671	128,021

ESTIMATED PRODUCE OF THE PRECEDING CROPS IN QUARTERS OR TONS IN EACH YEAR FROM 1870 TO 1879.

YEAR.	WHEAT. Quarters.	OATS. Quarters.	POTATOES. Tons.	FLAX. Tons.
1870, . .	754,261	7,559,303	4,218,445	30,771
1871, . .	705,939	7,410,814	2,793,641	12,919
1872, . .	609,831	6,654,456	1,805,827	17,089
1873, . .	469,563	6,912,765	2,683,060	19,843
1874, . .	687,625	7,159,034	3,551,605	18,037
1875, . .	552,417	8,203,707	3,512,884	22,430
1876, . .	481,815	7,648,774	4,154,785	27,141
1877, . .	452,672	6,374,180	1,757,275	22,213
1878, . .	549,916	6,814,697	2,526,504	22,175
1879, . .	419,750	5,436,420	1,113,676	19,144

SALE OF LAND TO TENANTS.

The sales to tenants under the Bright clauses of the Irish Land Act of 1870, in which charging orders to the Board of Works, for advances to enable them to purchase, made were, 71 in 1876, 84 in 1877, 129 in 1878, and 42 in 1879, for £60,919, £82,660, £117,421, and £43,250 respectively. (See Thom's Official Directory, 1881.)

The following is a copy of the lease given by Mr. William Scully to his tenants on the Ballycohey estate, in 1868, and which they were bound to accept under pain of eviction:

"First. That he, the said tenant, his heirs, executors, administrators, or assigns, will pay the said rent to the said landlord, his heirs, executors, administrators and assigns, at the time and times, and in the manner hereinbefore mentioned.

"And will also pay the entire of all poor rates, and county cess, and all other rates, taxes, duties, and assessments whatsoever (quit-rent and rent charge in lieu of tithes only excepted) now due, or hereafter to become due or payable out, or in respect of, the said demised lands and premises or any part thereof; and shall not make or retain, or be entitled to or require any deduction or allowance whatsoever out of the rent aforesaid or otherwise from the said landlord, his heirs, executors, administrators, or assigns, for or in respect of such poor rates, county cess, and other rates, taxes, duties, and assessments, or any of them, or any part thereof.

"Secondly. That the said tenant, his executors, administrators, or assigns, or any of tehm, or any person whosoever, claiming or deriving from, through, by, or under him, them, or any of them, shall not at any time, or in any event, have any claim, right, or title to, and shall not at any time, or in any event, claim to have, or to be entitled to, emblements, or any customary, or waygoing, or other crop, or proportion of a crop which shall be growing upon the said demised lands or premises, or any part thereof, at the end or determination of this demise, or of the tenancy hereby created, or any right or benefit thereof, or any compensation therefor, or have or claim to have any right of possession, holding or occupation of the said land and premises or of any part thereof, in lieu of emblements, or in lieu of the right to emblements, or of such customary, waygoing or other crop, or proportion of a crop, any statute, usage, custom, right, or thing to the contrary in any wise notwithstanding.

"Thirdly. That the said tenant, his executors, administrators and assigns, or any of them will not cut down, lop, prune, or grub up any tree growing or to grow on said demised lands, and will not cut down any hedge thereon without properly guarding such hedge from injury. And that he and they will dig up and cut down all docks, thistles, and other weeds which shall be on said demised lands during the continuance of this demise before they go to seed, and that he and they will, during the continuance of this demise, well and sufficiently preserve, repair, and keep the said demised lands and premises and the trees, fences, hedges, ditches, drains, water-courses, buildings, gates, and all fixtures and improvements, with the appurtenances which now are, or at any time during this demise shall be erected or made, or shall be thereon, in good and tenantable order, repair, and condition; and at the end or determination of this demise or of the tenancy hereby created, will quit and deliver up to the said landlord, his heirs or assigns, or to some or one of them, the possession of the said demised lands and premises, with the appurtenances in like good tenantable order, repair, and condition. And that on the first day of December, first day of March, first day of June, or first day of September, which shall next follow the expiration of twenty-one days (Sundays included) from the service by, or on the part of, the said landlord, his heirs and assigns, or any of them upon the said tenant, his executors, administrators, or assigns, or any of them of a notice requiring the delivery to the said landlord, his heirs or assigns, or any of them, of the possession of the said demised lands and premises, this demise and the tenancy hereby created shall determine and the said landlord, his heirs or assigns shall be entitled to the immediate possession of the said demised lands and premises with the appurtenances, and the said tenant, his executors, administrators or assigns, or any person claiming or deriving from, through, by, or under him, them, or any of them, shall not, nor shall any one or more of them, have any power, right or option either at law or in equity, to continue to hold or occupy the said lands or premises, or any part thereof, for any longer time, any law, custom or thing to the contrary notwithstanding.

"Fourthly. That the said last-mentioned notice, and also any other notice under these presents, may be served upon the said tenant, his executors, administrators, or assigns, or any of them, either personally, or by leaving the same at the usual or last known place or places of abode in Ireland of him, them, or any of them, or by posting same upon the door of a dwelling-house (if any) situated on the said demised lands and premises, or by posting same on some conspicuous part of such dwelling-house adjacent to the entrance thereto. And any notice which shall be so left or posted, shall be deemed to be served on the same tenant, his executors, administrators, or assigns within the true intent and meaning of these presents.

"Fifthly. That the said tenant, his executors, administrators, or assigns shall not, during the continuance of this demise, assign, mortgage, alien, demise, underlet, or set in conacre, or for any crop or crops, or bequeath or devise by will or testament, or by any codicil thereto, or in any manner dispose of the said lands and premises, or any part thereof, without first obtaining the consent in writing, for that purpose, of the said landlord, his heirs, or assigns, signed by him or them.

"Sixthly. That the said tenant, his executors, administrators, or assigns, or any of them, shall not, nor will, during the continuance of this demise, erect or make, or permit or suffer to be erected or made, on the said demised lands and premises, any dwelling-house, or other house, building, hedge, ditch, fence, dyke, or drain whatever, except such as he and they shall from time to time be previously authorized to erect or make by the said landlord, his heirs or assigns, in writing signed by him or them.

"Seventhly. That the said tenant, his executors, administrators, or assigns, or any of them, or any person claiming or deriving from, through, by, or under him, them, or any of them, will not burn, or permit or suffer to be burned, the soil or surface of the said demised lands and premises, or any part or parts thereof. And will not till or break up or change from grass, or permit or suffer to be tilled or broken up or changed from grass in any one year, more than one-fourth part of the entire acreable contents of the said demised lands; and will not meadow, or permit or suffer to be meadowed, in any one year, more than one-——th part of the entire acreable contents of the said demised lands. And will, during the continuance of this demise, carefully and effectually protect and preserve all wild fowl and game of every kind in and upon the said lands and premises for the exclusive use and sporting of the said landlord, his heirs and assigns, and of all persons authorized by him or them to sport thereon.

"It is hereby declared and agreed that the said tenant, his executors, administrators, and assigns paying all arrears of the said rent, and performing all the covenants and agreements herein on his and their part contained, shall be at liberty to surrender this lease and the possession of the said lands and premises, with the fixtures and appurtenances in good tenantable order, repair, and condition, as aforesaid, on any 1st day of December, 1st day of March, 1st day of June, or 1st day of September in any year, upon giving a previous notice in writing of 21 days (Sundays included) to that effect to the said landlord, his heirs or assigns, either personally or by leaving such notice at his or their dwelling-house with any member of his or their family aged sixteen years or upwards, or with his or their servant aged sixteen years or upwards. And the said tenant hereby surrenders all former leases, agreements, proposals and contracts of every kind of or concerning the said lands and premises, or any part or parts thereof.

" In witness whereof, etc."

Agrarian Outrages

Since 1844 have averaged five thousand each year. In 1845 the number was 8,104; in 1846, 12,382; in 1847, 20,980; in 1848, 14,430; in 1849, 14,980; and in 1850, 10,639. In 1870 the number was 1,359. The number of evictions in the famine years was enormously large; hence the large proportion of outrages. In 1874, '75, '76, and '77, the evictions averaged 503 yearly; in 1878 there were 743; in 1879, 1,098; and for the first part of 1880, 1,696; many of the families being restored by the protest and vigilance of the Land League. The number of outrages for 1880 was in much smaller ratio to the number of evictions than in any of the preceding years. By the statistics of the Irish Registrar General it appears that there were thirteen thousand evictions during the past ten years.

See Mr. Parnell's speech in the House of Commons, January, 1881.

The following Tabular Statement gives the number of factories in operation in Ireland, and the number of men and women employed:—

FACTORIES.	Number of Factories.	PERSONS EMPLOYED.		
		Males.	Females.	Total.
Cotton factories,	8	1,183	1,892	3,075
Woollen factories,	60	782	724	1,506
Worsted factories,	1	3	9	12
Flax factories,	149	18,323	41,993	60,316
Hemp factories,	4	221	120	341
Jute factories,	11	479	1,615	2,094
Silk factories,	2	290	110	400
Total,	235	21,281	46,463	67,744

See "Statesman's Year Book" (Frederick Martin).

For sketch of De Beaumarchais, see Beaumarchais et son temps, par M. Lomènie, and L'histoire de France, par M. Guizot.

Abstract of Miss Parnell's Speech in Claremorris.

Rev. Chairman, Ladies and Gentlemen: — The second resolution has been intrusted to me to propose, and I hope you will keep as quiet as possible, because I want to make myself heard. There is no use taking the trouble of talking at all unless you are listened to.

Resolved, That we hereby enter our public protest against the arrest of Michael Davitt; and to avenge his imprisonment in a way worthy of the noble spirit of Christian women by staying the evil effects of tyranny and legalized violence, we call on the women of Ireland to form in each parish a branch of the Ladies' Irish National Land League, and thus at once call into existence the last public expressed wish of the imprisoned patriot.

Before speaking to the resolution, I wish to thank the ladies of Claremorris for their beautiful reception, and to express the pleasure it gives me to hear the national music of Ireland played by the excellent bands of Mayo. Whatever the English government has succeeded in doing, it has not succeeded in crushing the Irish genius for music. There is just one point I want to call your attention to — it is about this movement of ours. We are not a political movement, but we are not a charitable movement either, because charity is understood to mean alms-giving, and this movement has nothing whatever to do with alms, which is understood by the word "charity." It is a relief movement. The money which we shall have to administer will be the money which has been subscribed by the people themselves, and intrusted to the Irish National Land League to help them when the emergency arose. Thus I hope that you will all remember our title is relief, and our work is relief, not charity. We don't want the people whom we help, to feel humiliated, or to feel as if they were getting money which they had no right to. They will have the best right in the world to everything they get. Now, I don't suppose you require me to tell you what the Irish Land League is. You know all about it, and probably you may know more about it than I do myself. You know also that for about twelve months the landlords of Ireland have not been getting as much rents as they claim to be entitled to, and they are very savage in consequence; and perhaps within the next six months they will get still less, and then they will get still more savage. Well, some other gentlemen are getting savage too—not Irish landlords. I will mention three of them—three Christian gentlemen. They are Mr. Gladstone, Mr. Forster, and honest John Bright. Well, the reason why they are savage is that the Irish people refuse to be satisfied with a mixture of buckshot and good intentions, instead of food and clothes; that they refuse to be pleased and happy when they are turned out of their homes in the dead of winter, and when they are robbed of all they possess; that they refuse to be pleased, and go on their knees and call Mr. Gladstone and Mr. Bright their friends; and so it is no longer possible for Mr. Gladstone, or Mr. Bright, or Mr. Forster, to parade themselves in Ireland as the friends of Ireland, and that is making them very savage. Well, now, what is it that they want to do? They are bringing in a bill—they are trying to pass a law—and it may be passed next week—which will enable the Lord Lieutenant of Ireland to put any man or woman in prison, and keep them there for a year and a half.

Very well. And how will they use this law? This is the way these Christian gentlemen intend to use this law. Whenever a landlord wants to evict a tenant, or whenever he wants to evict a large number of tenants, he will apply to the Lord Lieutenant of Ireland to put any man or woman in prison whom he thinks will be likely to give help to those evicted tenants. You know that heretofore the Land League has worked in this way: when tenants have been evicted, the Land League has given money to the local leagues,— to the treasurers, presidents, and secretaries of the local leagues,— to help evicted families so that they might not starve, and public opinion has been called in to prevent any one else taking the farms.

Well, now, you see it will disorganize the relief of evicted tenants very much if the landlord has it in his power, before he carries out his eviction — if he has it in his power to put in prison the men whose duty it is to provide for those evicted families; and it is for the purpose of supplying the place of those men in carrying on the work of relief that we have been called into existence by Michael Davitt. Mr. Forster, Mr. Gladstone, and Mr. Bright hope that when the Habeas Corpus Act is suspended, the relief branch of the work of the Irish National Land League will fall into confusion, and the tenants who are evicted may be left to want, and that the families of persons imprisoned may be left to want and starvation. That is what those leagues are organized to prevent or to remedy. (See "Connaught Telegraph," February, 1881.)

By the census of 1861, Irish-born persons formed over twenty-one per cent. of the colonists in Western Australia, over eighteen per cent. in Queensland, over sixteen per cent. in Victoria, in New South Wales over fifteen per cent., ten per cent. in South Australia, over thirteen per cent. in Upper Canada, and nearly a sixth of the population in New Zealand. We have seen that these colonies enjoy "responsible governments."

EXTRACT FROM A LETTER OF HIS EMINENCE CARDINAL MANNING, TO EARL GREY, IN 1868:

In England the traditions of centuries, the steady growth of our mature social order, the ripening of our agriculture and industry, the even distribution and increase of wealth have reduced the relation of landlord and tenant to a fixed, though it be an unwritten law, by which the rights of both are protected. Our land laws may be enforced in the courts, and thereby have the force of law. English landlords as a rule live on their estates. Their lands are their homes. English tenants are protected by the mightiest power that ever ruled a Christian country — a power which controls the Legislature, dictates the laws, and guides even the sovereignty of the Crown,—the force of a vigilant, watchful, ubiquitous public opinion. But in Ireland none of these things are so. In one-fourth of Ireland there are land laws, or rather land customs, which protect the tenant. In three-fourths of Ireland there are neither laws nor customs. The tenants are tenants-at-will. Over a vast part of Ireland the landlords are absentees. The mitigating and restraining influence of the lords of the soil, which in England and in every civilized country do more to correct the excesses of the agents, speculators, and traffickers, and to temper legal rights with equity and moderation, are hardly to be found. . . . The tenant-at-will may be put out for any cause, not only for non-payment of rent, or waste of land, or bad farming, or breach of covenant, if such can be supposed to exist, all of which would bear a color of justice, but for the personal advantage of the landlord arising from the tenants' improvements, for political influence, for caprice, for any passing reason or no reason, assigned or assignable, which can arise in minds conscious of absolute and irresponsible power. . . . If the events which have passed in Ireland since 1810 had passed in England, the public opinion of the latter country would have imperiously compelled the Legislature to turn our land customs into acts of Parliament. If any sensible proportion of the people of English counties were to be seen moving down upon the Thames for embarkation to America, and dropping by the roadside from hunger and fever, and it had been heard by the wayside that they were tenants-at-will, evicted for any cause whatsoever, the public opinion of the country would have risen to render impossible the repetition of such absolute and irresponsible exercise of legal rights. If five millions, *i. e.*, one-fourth of the British people, had either emigrated in a mass by reason of discontent, misery, or eviction, or had died by fever and by famine since the year 1848, the whole land system of England would have been modified so as to render the return of such a national danger impossible forever. But both these suppositions have been verified in Ireland. It is precisely because these suppositions have been verified in Ireland that we are now face to face with a most dangerous agitation. There is now a loud and bitter cry against landlordism, and the due distinction between bad and good landlords is often disregarded; but it is undeniable that this anti-landlord agitation, so far as it goes, is a reaction against the unprincipled extortion and the anti-national attitude of a large proportion of Irish land owners. The late Lord Derby had the truth and courage to charge the Irish landlords with insatiable avarice; and so notorious was this spirit of avarice, that Walker, the compiler of the best of dictionaries, defined the word rack-rent to mean the rent usually extorted by Irish landlords from their tenants.

The gross rental of the Irish tenant farmers is estimated at £15,000,000. The reduction proposed by the Land League would lessen the amount by a third. This the landlords object to, notwithstanding the changed conditions superinduced by defective crops, and lower prices for all commodities in the market, brought about by foreign competition. English tenants suffer from the same causes, but their status is materially different from that of the Irish. In England a yearly tenant can only be evicted on a year's notice, to take effect at the expiration of the taking. He is then entitled to compensation for all unexhausted improvements, and at the beginning of the taking is provided with dwelling-house, barn, outhouses, etc., at the expense of the landlord. The following letter gives evidence of the effect of changed conditions in England:—

The Rent Question.

13 South-Road, Birmingham, Feb. 24, 1881.

To the Editor:

Sir,—As we are now entering on another phase of the rent question between landlords and tenants under the influence of a Coercion Act for Ireland, I think it my duty to place before the land-owning class of my native country the position and prospects of landlord and tenant in England. Since I came to live here, I have endeavored to discover the reason why so much that is wrong and unjust exists in Ireland, whilst the land question is being so calmly and quietly discussed and decided in England. Through the great kindness of a local gentleman who has taken much interest in this subject, and in whose hands are unchallengeable proofs in support of the statements, I am enabled to give instances of the reductions of rent and a few statements as to agricultural holdings. I purposely refrain from close particulars of identification; but the facts are given. This information may cause some Irish owners to pause in what I consider a suicidal career of eviction and extermination, and in the further exactions of rents contracted under circumstances now forever passed away, and which will never again return to the agricultural classes, whether landlord or tenant, in the United Kingdom of Great Britain and Ireland.

Warwickshire. — One farm, in the occupation of present family for 150 years, is now surrendering to the landlord. The original rent was 10s. per acre; present rent, 38s. 6d.; re-offered to tenant at 20s. per acre, who declined to pay over 16s., and has accepted a large farm in a neighboring county at 18s. per acre. In the county generally, stiff lands on fresh take a considerable reduction of rents; in one instance, after a large expenditure in improvements, was re-let at 35 per cent. reduction of rent. In other portions of the county, lands let at 30s., reduced to 20s., and some so low as from 25s. to 10s. per acre. There is a very great proportion (in some places four-fifths) of lands unlet.

Oxfordshire. — In this county, on one estate, there are 1,500 acres unoccupied. In other districts many farms are vacant, and others let at merely nominal rents; in many cases, half rent is accepted to keep the tenant on the farm. Farms let at 40s. can be had for 30s.; some lately let at 20s. are now at 10s. per acre.

Bedfordshire. — New lettings are concluded at 75, 50, and 25 per cent. reduction. There has been one instance of refusal to pay even the rates, because the occupying tenant now pays no rent, though the former rent was 36s. per acre. In parts of this county laborers on agricultural holdings are in a most lamentable and precarious condition.

Essex. — In this county lands appear to be let at a nominal rent for one year, the following rent showing reductions of 40 to 50 per cent. on original lettings. One well-known case of nearly 400 acres is let at 5s. per acre, being 75 per cent. reduction.

Gloucestershire. — A farm let at £40 per annum was originally held at £80.

Shropshire. — Great numbers of tenants gave notice of surrender; those who remained received reductions of rent equal to 25, 15, and 10 per cent.; others, temporary allowances, and some 50 per cent. reduction on former rent.

Huntingdonshire.— Good lands are difficult to re-let at valuations equal to original rent, from 40s. per acre now reduced to 25s. or 20s.; and lands let at 30s. are offered at 15s. per acre. Cold clay lands, usual rent 30s., will now be re-let, if any tenants can be found, at 10s. and 7s. per acre. Some tenants are allowed to remain merely to take care of the farm. The value of the fee-simple of land in this district reduced from £45 to £30 per acre. Many farms have been offered for sale without obtaining a single bid.

Leicestershire.— Where a heavy outlay has been made by landlord, a large farm has been re-let at 30s., the former rent being 34s. per acre. Another instance: a very large farm, recently held at 42s. per acre, has been re-let, a large portion at 30s., the remaining portion at 20s. per acre. These instances in the immediate vicinity of large industrial centres. Lands let at 35s. are now re-let at 20s. per acre; other farms, original rent 52s., now re-let at 40s. per acre. One large farm, re-valued every fifteen years, the tenant farmed so well, had his rent raised during forty-five years occupation from 20s. to 40s. per acre. This farm cannot now be re-let at the offered rental of 22s. 6d. per acre.

West Norfolk.— But few changes have been

made on the best chalk soils, but re-lettings are equal to from 15 to 25 per cent. reduction. On sandy soils many farms are unoccupied. In the marsh land districts there have been considerable reductions and re-lettings at nominal rents for one year. In the Fen lands reductions are equal to from 25*s.* to 20*s.* per acre.

Now, sir, these facts and figures from over a small portion of rich and powerful England speak with trumpet-tongue to the landlords of Ireland, and are more powerful arguments than any platform oratory which we can command; and I now commend this letter to the careful consideration of landlord and tenant, and also to the earnest consideration of the manufacturing and mercantile community of Ireland and England. The present depressed condition of agriculture having no small influence upon the general prosperity of all industrial affairs, my desire is that the eyes of all concerned may be truly enlightened to the condition of our country before it is too late, and that the dictates of humanity and charity may be listened to and fulfilled by all classes so deeply interested in a fair and just settlement of the present unhappy and disastrous position of the tenantry of Ireland.

I am, with much respect, yours very truly,

JOHN W. MULLIN.

www.ingramcontent.com/pod-product-compliance
Lightning Source LLC
Chambersburg PA
CBHW021939240426
43669CB00047B/574